Mother Why Are You Weeping?

Mother Why Are You

Weeping?

Michelle Geter

Laurice Brickus

LaChae Morton

CHARIS GRACE
PUBLISHING

Mother Why Are You Weeping?

Charis Grace Publishing LLC

CHARIS GRACE
PUBLISHING

charisgracepublishing@gmail.com

Place of publication: Virginia Beach, Virginia

For Global Distribution

Printed in the United States of America

Paperback ISBN: 979-8-218-30461-4

Library of Congress Control Number: 2023920905

Mother, Why Are You Weeping?

Weeping- "expressing grief, sorrow, or any overwhelming emotion by shedding tears: weeping multitudes. Tearful; weepy: a weeping fit. Tending or liable to cry; given to crying."[1]

"When Jesus saw her weeping and saw the other people wailing with her, a deep anger welled up within him, and he was deeply troubled… They told him, 'Lord, come and see.' Then Jesus wept"
(NLT, John 11:33-35)

---

[1] Dictionary.com. (n.d.). Weeping. In *Dictionary.com Dictionary*. Retrieved October 28, 2023, from https://www.dictionary.com/browse/weeping

Contents

Dedicated to the Weepers

Michelle

I dedicate this book to mothers, fathers, siblings, friends, husbands, wives, and anyone who has found themselves weeping over the loss of a loved one. A loss of a loved one does not necessarily mean a physical death, but a separation of a relationship; a divorce. The absence of a loved one can cause you to weep. There are several reasons why situations and circumstances in life may cause you to weep. Let me list a few.

The loss of a loved one; past regrets; death; grief; a runaway child; an abducted loved one. A family member addicted to some type of substance, or suffering from suicide, mental disorders, or incarceration. Being overwhelmed with joy; the birth of a child; a marriage proposal; fear and anxiety; loneliness; frustration. What about when you receive that call that your child has been diagnosed with what the doctor says is an incurable disease? When you find out your toddler choked on a piece of candy and passed away? Sickness and disease; loss of employment; family matters; deep, deep hurt.

Through life's journey, there are many circumstances that can make you weep for days, months, and even years. I am sure that at one time or another, you may have wept for one of the reasons listed. If not, as my mother would say, "Just keep on living." What about when life throws that curveball at you? One that you are not able to dodge or duck, and you find yourself wondering, "What happened? Why me? Why now? Why did this situation have to happen?" It is those unexpected events that have you weeping and crying out for somebody, anybody, to help you. When you get that knock at the door, or that phone call that puts you in a fetal position. How do you stand when you no longer want to stand? How do you smile when you have nothing to smile about? How about when everything has been taken from you and you find yourself homeless?

As we look around today, there are so many people that are struggling. As I drive to work in the morning, I see that woman sleeping on top of a car tire. No longer do I look from a place of judging that woman, but I shed a tear and I whisper a prayer. My soul cries out because that could have been me. When you see that father who has a look of despair; that father who is on the bench at 5:00 a.m. because he has nowhere to go, and all his belongings are on the bench next to him, send love over judgment. As you read this book, you will understand that I know your pain. I feel what you feel. When words cannot even explain what is going on inside. Yes, it happened to me. A seat that I had to sit in. I did not sign up for it, but I was chosen by God to take a seat. God knew I could handle losing my son without throwing in the towel or turning my back on Him. I was chosen to stand in His strength and not my own. When I am weak, yes, God is strong (see 2 Corinthians 12:10). This scripture really came alive in my life.

The moment I decided to write this book—even though I thought I was all cried out—as I began to put words to the paper, I began to cry. I began to feel that piercing pain in my heart. God, please heal those wounded areas in my life that I have not allowed You to deal with before. Help me to heal, so the memory of the pain does not continue to affect me, as if it just happened yesterday. I am tired of crying and hurting like I do. Lord, will this pain ever go away?

Before telling my story, I heard several times that I should write a book. But I wondered to myself, "Who would want to hear what I have to say? What makes my story any different from the next mother? I am not the first mother who loss her child, and I will not be the last. What do I have to say that can or will help someone else?" I didn't realize that writing would be another part of my healing process, and once I received complete healing and wholeness, then I would be able to help someone else. I remember a song that says, "If I could help someone along the way, then my living would not be in vain."[2] But I am saying that if I can help someone else, then my son's death was not in vain.

For years, I even struggled with a name for a book. "If I did decide to write, what would the title of the book be?" I was not sure what I would title the book until March 22, 2023. I was at church, praying, around 8:00 a.m. Apostle Melvin Thompson, III called the leadership team and church, All Nations HBG, to a twenty-four-hour prayer. We all had to take at least one hour and pray. I cannot explain it, but I began to weep nonstop that morning before work. Apostle Thompson had prayer points posted up at the church, and I read all of them. Worship music was playing, and I went to the altar to read all the prayer points. I got stuck at the prayer point for gun violence, murder, and suicide. All I could do was weep before the Lord. I tried to stop crying, but I could not. The tears just kept coming, running down my eyes like a waterfall. I heard, "Mother, why are you weeping? Why are you weeping?" I knew that would be the title of my book, as well as another part of the process to my

---

[2] Mahalia Jackson. (1964). If I Can Help Somebody.

healing. I knew God wanted me whole so I could encourage others who have experienced the loss of a child.

Before writing this book, I would encounter other mothers and fathers who lost their child or children or were dealing with difficult situations with their children. To see a parent weeping over the loss of a child, and to know exactly what they are going through because you have walked in those same shoes, but sometimes, you yourself do not have the words to say to that parent, even though you have experienced a similar situation.

How can you tell a mother that everything is going to be okay, when it appears as if there is no hope? Or to a mother who has not lost only one child, but two, only a couple of years apart? What about to that parent who just loss a child to gun violence and one to the judicial system? That parent that just loss their child in a car accident? What do you do when that mother gives you that look, that stare, and you can see in her eyes that she has stopped living? When you see the pain, the grief, the guilt written all over their face? When you embrace that mother that has turned to some type of substance to numb the pain. How do you embrace that mother whose son has been given time for taking a life? What about that mother who sends her child off to college and they end up incarcerated for defending a friend?

What about that mother who loss her child and then she got diagnosed with Cancer?

Sitting in service one morning, I was asked to go give a sister a hug. Mother, why are you weeping? "Lord, what do I say?" I began to embrace this sister. I could not say a word, but I held her in my arms. I could hear the words to tell her to release what she had been holding onto. I whispered a prayer and asked God to heal the deep hurt that she was carrying around, to free her up. The sister began to open up and told me that she had been walking around with pain from thirty years ago. Help! Lord, I feel the same pain that some of them are feeling or experiencing. All I can do is embrace them with a hug and whisper a prayer. Lord, help. Some of them I need to cry with, and others I need to stand in the gap and pray for, because if anyone knows, I know.

God, why did I have to experience this? Why does it seem as if there is a hole in my heart, leaking and tearing it into so many pieces? I often ask myself, "Will the pain I feel ever go away?" Lord, I just need the grace, strength, and peace of mind to live through this. One day at a time, one month at a time, and one year at a time.

I do not know how Mary did it. I cannot imagine, as a mother, how Mary could watch them crucify her son, Jesus Christ. Mary had to watch them brutally beat her child. It is one thing to know that your child was murdered or killed, but to be there when it happened? I have no words. But I do know that it took a lot of strength, because we know, as parents, that any time anyone does something to one of our children, our first instinct is to react. It is natural to want to get them back for hurting one of our babies. Mary is a great display of strength.

Numb November

Michelle

As I began to reflect over the last seventeen years, I found myself sitting alone in my seat and trying to figure out how I became bruised, broken, spiritually bent over, bound, and muzzled. I had no clue as to what the Kingdom was all about. I thought I was just getting saved and going to heaven; I had no idea about being called into ministry or anything about the anointing. When I got saved, I felt at that time that God was telling me to just be myself. The scripture that I memorized was Mathew 6:33, *"But seek ye first the kingdom of God, and his righteousness; and all these things shall be added unto you"* (KJV). I guess I can say that it was the first time God spoke to me. My experience of being numb occurred on November 19, 2006, when I accepted the call into ministry, and I preached my initial sermon. As I looked out into the crowd, I noticed someone was missing. My oldest daughter LaChae was unable to attend, as she was away at school, but Laurice and Maurice Jr. were sitting out in the crowd, supporting their mother. LaChae wrote a poem, and Laurice read it aloud.

"For Mom"

You've always been there for us.

Keeping us straight and whipping our butts.

Always pushing for the best,

and never settling for anything less.

There were times we wanted to quit when something was too hard,

You would always say something like, "You can do all things because you've got the favor of God."

You're always willing to help others in need.

You're a beautiful woman, everyone who knows you can see,

the type of person I'd like to grow up to be.

Now it's our turn to be there for you.

You will deliver God's message and we will help you through.

We will just remind you of everything you always say,

"You can do it. You will be okay."

Remember this is only the first, there will be many more.

To sum it all up we just want to say,

We wouldn't be Michelle's kids if we didn't say we love you today.

My children were still trying to get used to the idea of their mother being saved and changing her life around. See, they had the opportunity to see the unsaved and the saved version of mom. LaChae, Laurice, and Maurice Jr. came up with their own truth or dare game and called it, "You Are Not One of Michelle's Kids if You Don't' Do This".… I am sure it tells you what our house was like. I can recall times when we would all be in one bed, playing games, laughing—we were happy. They would all pile in my bed, and we would watch TV together, enjoying one another and talking. I did not have extra money left over after paydays, so it was not like we could go out and do other things. I was trying to grow up, and I did not want to ask my parents, even though they would have given money to me. We had indoor activities. I remember times counting coins, and one day it had snowed, and Maurice Jr. and I walked to the store. I had enough change to buy hamburger, spaghetti, and sauce, to be able to cook spaghetti, a meal that would last us for a few days. I also thought about a time when LaChae would braid hair and babysit to make money, and I had to sit her down to tell my child that I needed her help. She made more money than me, braiding hair and babysitting. We helped one another during the rough times.

Looking out into the crowd, it made me feel so proud to have them there that night. I was nervous, scared, and anxious; wanting for it all to be over, but wanting that reassurance from my dad, that everything was going to be all right. I was daddy's little girl, even at the age of thirty-eight. There were days that I would get off work, go to my parents' house, and lay in the bed next to my father, Mack. Or if my mother, Rose, were in the bed, I would lay at the bottom of the bed with the two of them. While my father watched the news, we would just talk about life and what happened throughout our day. My father would watch Jeopardy and Wheel of Fortune, and I would listen to him call out most of the answers to the questions being asked. Some days, I would just go lay in the bed in the bedroom that I grew up in as a teenager and take a nap before going home. I felt peace and protection at my parents' home. It was a room full of smoke, but it did not matter; I was spending time with my Daddy.

I was grateful for all those who came out to support me that evening, even for the spectators. The Mother of the Church, who was also the District Missionary, Mother Allen, and The Superintendent, Elder DR Gilmore, who was once my pastor, even showed up to support and share a few words of encouragement. What I really wanted was to see my father's face in the crowd looking back at me, letting me know he was proud of me. I finally started to grow up and get my life together. My message was titled, "Filled with Compassion," taken from Luke 10:25-37, the *Parable of the Good Samaritan*. After it was all over,

I greeted everyone and thanked them for coming out to support me, especially my family that traveled to Pennsylvania to surprise me and support me. I rushed to my parents' house, wondering why my father had not shown up. I was a little disappointed, I must say. I rushed up the stairs to my parents' bedroom and I sat on the bed next to my dad. Before I could get a word out, my father looked into my eyes and apologized for not showing up to support me. But he promised that he would be there the next time I spoke. In my heart, I knew something must be going on or something was wrong with my dad, because my father always showed up to events to support and help as much as he could.

I remember one day, I went to a parent-teacher conference at school for LaChae, and my father met me at the school. I looked around her classroom that day and noticed that I was the youngest parent in the room. It was not until then that I realized that I was a single parent. Everyone was coupled up, but I was there with my father. I never saw myself as a single mom, because of the love and support I received from my parents. I was single, but not divorced. LaChae, Laurice, and Maurice Jr. would ask my parents for things before they would come to ask me. My parents were their parents too, instead of their grandparents. I never had to worry about a babysitter or daycare or them being harmed. I had wonderful parents. My mother would often say that I gave birth to them, but they were her kids, and she meant it.

My dad loved me through my mistakes, as he waited for me to grow up and get it together. My father told me when I was younger—before I had my first child or even married my first husband—that if someone is walking down the street and if they are not going in the same direction that I am headed in, then I should cross over the street and keep on walking. I did not get the revelation of what my father was saying to me until I was thirty-three years old. My dad saw what I could not see or did not want to see in the men I married or brought home. I cannot tell you how many times I walked down the same street instead of crossing over. He allowed me to make the mistakes and loved me through it all.

My father and younger brother, Mack Jr., talked that night, because he and my nephew, Aren, would be leaving early in the morning to return home. That next morning, about one or two hours after they left to head home, my dad received a phone call that a deer ran into the SUV and totaled my brother's vehicle. Thank God that their lives were spared. My father and I drove to go pick them up and returned back to my parents' house. Later that day, my brother and father would sit down and talk, and he would give my brother his truck so they could return home. The next morning, my brother and nephew would head out in my father's truck.

A customer at work gave me two tickets to a Pittsburgh Steelers' and Ravens' game. I was so excited, but I did not want to choose between who I would take, my son or my father, because both were the two most important men in my life. So, I gave my father and son the tickets. On Sunday, November 26, 2006, I drove them to Baltimore to see their favorite NFL team play. Steeler Nation all day! My father and son were so excited all the way down. They had their Steeler gear on, along with their Terrible Towels. It was the first and last NFL live game they would ever attend. My father was out of breath when he came to the car to return home. I watched him closely but did not say anything. But I wondered in my mind, "What is going on with my dad?" I had never seen him like that before. He did not show up at church and now, he seems so exhausted after just walking to the car. I thought he was upset because it was his first NFL game and the Steelers Lost 0-27 that day.

Ten days later, after accepting the call into ministry, on November 29th at 11:15-11:30pm, I was awakened out of my sleep from a call from my mom. She was panicking on the other end of the phone, not knowing what to do, but trying to get the words out.

She uttered over the phone, "YOUR DAD IS HAVING A HEART ATTACK! Something is wrong with your dad; something is wrong with Mack." I said back to my mom, "My father is having a heart attack?" I hung up the phone and raced to my parents' house. I prayed all the way there. "Lord, help my father, do not let my father die." I felt that gut feeling, tightening in my stomach. I didn't even think to call the ambulance to have them meet me there. I knew my mom was not thinking clearly enough to call 911. I rushed to my parents' house, and I heard my father gurgle and take his last breath. I called the ambulance, and they asked me to perform CPR on my father. I was scared, nervous, and didn't understand, but I knew in my heart that my father was gone. He was not there, so why would they want me to go through the motions? My dad's eyes had already rolled into the back of his head, and he just had that stare. I knew he was not there.

The paramedics arrived and they went through the motions. I watched them carry my father down the stairs and out of the house. Do not ask me how, but we beat the ambulance to the hospital. They left before we did, how could that be? River Rescue was at the bottom of the hill of my parents' house on Cameron Street. When we arrived at the hospital, they asked the family to wait in the family waiting room. I called my aunt and uncle and my brother. I knew it was not going to be good news.

The doctor came out at 12:00 a.m. on November 30, 2006, and pronounced my father deceased. My entire world went numb that day. I was daddy's little girl. The man that I loved, looked up to, respected, and who loved me no matter what, was gone. Lord, how could this be? I answered the call, I said, "YES," Lord, and now, ten days later, you take my father from me? NO! Why now? Why, God?

On November 30,1985, my father retired from the military, and we moved to his hometown in Pennsylvania. Twenty-one years later, on the same date my father retired from the military, he passed away. Why now? God, what are you saying to me? I had so many unanswered questions racing through my mind. I took my mother home; my sister, Joyce, and older brother, Tony, met us at my parents' house. I called my youngest brother, Mack Jr., to tell him our father was gone. My brother was silent. He was in disbelief. Mack Jr. said that God spared his and his son's life a few weeks ago but took our father's. I was so numb; I just began to weep. My mother just kept busy. It was as if she froze, and she did not say a word. Is she even processing what is going on? I never saw her cry.

One of the hardest things I had to do was go home and tell my children, Laurice and Maurice Jr., that their grandfather was gone. Grandpa is what they all called him. I called my niece,

Squirt, to tell her that Mack, my dad, was dead. She met me at my house, and we went into my house together to tell my children. I remember waking Laurice and Maurice Jr. up and telling them that I had something I needed to tell them. When I said the words, "Grandpa had a heart attack and died," I remember the screams and the cries like it was yesterday. Next, I had to call LaChae, who was away at college, to tell her that grandpa was gone. The scream was piercing.

My father stood in the gap for their fathers, who were not present in their lives. Our lives would never be the same. My father made the difference and kept them on track. My children had a respect for my father, and they never wanted to disappoint him. I do not know how LaChae did it, but the next morning, before I could lay down to try to get some sleep, she was coming through the door. They all went into full speed to make all the service arrangements for my father. I was present, but I was not present. I was so hurt, angry, and going through the motions. My best friend was gone, and I felt completely lost; bruised, bent over, with a huge crack in my heart.

I remember my mother going through the house and getting rid of everything that represented my father. I was thinking, "Lord, what is she doing? Why? How could she be acting as if my father did not exist? Is this how she is dealing with the pain and grief?" I was silently crying on the inside. I remember the day of the service; I had to watch my children cry. My mother sat motionless and my grandmother, who they called Granny Lover, pushed her walker to the front of the church, bent over my father's casket, weeping and calling my father's name, "Mack, Mack, Mack, no, not Mack." The women who I knew, that had a strong relationship with God, who prayed for the entire family, was asking God why? A mother who must bury her child. This was a loss that was unexpected. Hurt—deep hurt. I could see the pain in my grandmother's eyes and the hurt on her face. I could just hear her, along with my children and family members, weeping. I was hurt, shocked, and numb. Six months later, my grandmother, Granny Lover, would transition to be with the Lord. The woman that I knew had prayed for me. It was another crack in my heart.

My father was a man who loved animals. Throughout my entire childhood, we had some type of pet: fish, dogs, and birds. I remember when I was young, when we moved from California and drove to Pennsylvania with two Doberman Pinschers in the car for five days to visit my grandmother. That is how much my father loved his pets. When my children were younger, my father had rabbits and a garden in the backyard of the house. My father taught my kids to fish, play dominos, and cards. My father loved to play Spades; he thought he was the Spades king until he had to play against me. I recall summer days when we would pull out the card table and play Spades in the backyard of my parents' house. If you played against me, trust and believe, you would be getting up a loser. I enjoy playing Spades and talking trash. My father loved birds, and we had and African Grey and a Half Moon parrot who loved my dad. The moment my father would get off work, the birds would come out of their cages. They competed for my father's attention. They would both call my father's name, Mack, and one would call my mother Rose. My father taught them to talk. It was not even a week or two after my father passed that the birds died. Life was different for us all.

Returning to work, I would cry all the way there. I would look at every work truck that looked like my father's, hoping to see my dad driving. "This was just a dream," I kept telling myself. I would see a man from the back that looked like my father, but when I saw the face, it was not him. I kept the recording to his voicemail for a year: "This is your dad, call me," he would say when he called to leave me a message. There were days that I did not even want to get out of bed. If I could talk to my father, I would tell him, "Dad! I finally grew up! I took care of Rose the best that I could. I miss you, and there are so many days I wish we could talk."

I remember my job wanted me to take a CPR class and, in the class, I got so emotional when they talked about heart attacks and giving CPR. I was just a wreck. A year later, on November 30, 2007, the company I work for—Exel (now DHL)—the account closed, and they did not have anywhere to place me, so I was laid off. "Lord, I do not know or understand what is going on," I said. The anniversary of my father's passing, and I get laid off? Who do I call? I cannot call my earthly father, because he is no longer here, so what God was teaching me was to learn to call and depend on Jesus. I did not know the Word of God that well. But I got a scripture and I stood on it the entire time I was laid off. The scripture was: *". . . Yet have I not seen the righteous forsaken, nor his seed begging bread"* (KJV, Psalm 37:25). It worked. I am here to tell you that I did better laid off than I did when I was working.

My children had mom at home when they got out of school each day, with a hot cooked meal on the table. God provided the entire time. My neighbor and my sister all rolled up into one, Sharon, was employed at the same account. She was laid off at the same time I was, and I tell you, God took great care of us. The only question our children had was when the two of us were going back to work. But it was during those times that I started knowing God for myself, learning to lean and depend on Him. I could call Him Provider and Comforter. I could no longer call on my dad to come help me out or come to my rescue. No, not this time. I had to really grow up. The entire time being out of work, God showed Sharon and I so much favor. You name it, Sharon had us doing it. God is a provider, and we never missed a beat nor a meal or bill. No one even knew that we were laid off. When I tell you that God had so many rams in the bushes waiting on us, I mean it. You never have to look like or sound like what you are going through or experiencing.

Six months after being laid off work, I was in church on Mother's Day, testifying of the goodness of Jesus and how good God is, and how He has kept my family while being laid off. Those in the congregation seemed shocked and surprised because every Sunday, I continued to show up, with a smile, blending in on the praise team and singing. Even though I could not sing, I did it to the glory of God. Elder Frison was my pastor at that time, and he asked if I would help serve in that area. I believe in obeying leadership, so I did as the man of God asked. I remember after church was over that Sunday, I headed to my parents' house after service to visit with my mother on Mother's Day. Little did I know that I would be spending Mother's Day in the emergency room.

This time, I was not asked to sit and wait in the family waiting area. I was a bit relieved, but still wondered what was going on with my mother. I sat there, waiting on the doctors to come but at the same time, I felt as if a muzzle was applied to my mouth, and it was being tightened again. I felt as if every time I would open my mouth to tell of the goodness of God, the muzzle was pulling my mouth shut a little more. I sat there, alone, weeping on the inside. It was Mother's Day, and I did not want to ruin anyone else's Mother Day. I called my children and told them I would be home later. I began to shut down, trying to understand why every time I opened my mouth or moved forward in the things of God, it felt as if a dart was thrown my way? Was I a target? I did not understand, nor did I feel like I had anyone to talk to or ask about these feelings I had going on inside of me. I was too young in my walk with Christ to really understand what spiritual warfare was all about. I did not know, while sitting in the waiting room, that for the next ten years, I would be my mother's caregiver. My mother would be my oldest daughter for the next ten years. My life took a major shift.

Can God trust you to take care of the person who birthed you and raised you? What do you do when the roles have been reversed? I was already taking care of my mother after the passing of my father, making sure her bills were paid and that she had everything she needed, and taking her to the stores. The doctors finally came in and to my surprise, my mother was diagnosed with Alzheimer's and Dementia, and she had suffered from a stroke. Lord, why did it seem that around the same time of each year something was happening within my family? I began to shut down and the muzzle got tighter, but I had to keep on moving, even though I did not understand. I did not realize it then, but my mom had Alzheimer's and Dementia when my father was alive.

Over the next few years, I would have several family members that would leave this Earth. I had a brother, Michael, that passed one week and after his homegoing service, I would turn around and have a homegoing service for my sister, Angie, who left us that same week. Lord, what is going on? Then it would be two uncles, two aunts, and a cousin. I was trying to keep it all together while my second marriage was falling apart. My children were not getting along. Lord, what is going on in my life?

November 19, 2014, brought the heaviest, hardest hit of them all. Do not get me wrong, every loss is a hit and affected me in an unusual way. Eight years ago, I answered the call, and I said, "Yes," to the Lord, not understanding what my "Yes" may require of me. *YES: Yield Everything Surrender.* November 19, 2014, would be the worst nightmare for me, LaChae, Laurice, and my family. My heart felt as though it was ripped out and torn into many pieces. My heart cracked in half. I was bent over, and I wept, wailed, screamed, cried, and then I got silent. I was unable to put language to what I was experiencing or feeling. How do I go on from here? Active depression sank in—I was actively going through the motions, but depressed.

My Vantage Point. . .

LaChae

So, I know my mom started off her story, but you would be surprised how two people that are going through the same life event have different perspectives. So, where do I start? I guess, in order for this story to really make any sense, I need to start by giving a little back story and telling you the role my grandfather played in my life.

So, Mack I. Thrasher was a very interesting man, and I'm happy I got to pick his brain and have him instill his principles in me before he passed away. Up until I was about twelve or thirteen years old, I was mainly raised by my grandparents, Mack and Rose. Everybody called my grandma by her name, Rose; kids, grandkids, it didn't matter, we all called her by her name for some reason. Honestly, I don't really know why, because we called my grandfather, grandpa… I know, it's confusing. I guess us grandkids just had a different level of respect, not really sure.

My mom, however, called him Mack. Whenever people that didn't know us or even other family members questioned why his kids called him by his name, he would say, "They know who I am." To him, they knew he was their father, so he wasn't concerned with the formalities.

Anyway, so my grandpa was my father figure. My parents had me pretty young, and my dad was in and out of jail most of my life, so my grandpa was *it* in terms of a father figure. I've never met anyone quite like my grandpa. He had a quiet demeanor and wouldn't be the loudest person in the room. However, when he entered, there was no mistaking he was there. He worked very hard and went to work every day. I barely recall him ever taking a day off. He loved black coffee and Winston cigarettes in the red pack. My grandma was a housewife, and she would wake up in the morning and make my grandpa's coffee for him. Now, my grandma's coffee-making skills were a little suspect. She probably made the worst coffee; it sometimes had coffee grounds floating around in it and was sometimes a little too strong. My grandpa never complained, though. He came downstairs, poured his coffee, and headed off to work each day, working about ten or more hours a day. When he came home, he would go straight to his room, where he would unwind for the evenings. My grandma would have his dinner ready, and she or one of us kids would take it upstairs to him. He ate whatever he was served, again with no complaints. He always watched the news and loved to keep himself educated on current events. He also watched TV shows like Jeopardy and would often get many of the answers correct.

As a kid, I remembered thinking how smart my grandpa was and if he knew all the answers, why he wouldn't go on the show. He had certain snacks that he liked, such as Wise butter popcorn and pork skins. He also had to have his Pepsi. He had a heart attack when I was much younger and after that, in an effort to switch up his habits, he switched to decaf Pepsi in the bronze can. He lived a very simple life, and he loved all of his grandkids.

As I mentioned, we lived with them, and he was so protective of us. Many times, when my mom would try to take me with her, my grandparents would tell her, "You go on now, but leave LaChae here." I was just fine with that too. My grandparents spoiled us so bad, it wasn't even funny. My early memories don't really go back before my sister, Laurice, was born, because we are only two and a half years apart. However, I remember clearly when my brother was born because there was a six-year difference. Rose was never one to sugar coat anything and she didn't believe in lying to kids, as she put it. So, needless to say, I knew exactly where my baby brother came from when he arrived. And it was my grandparents that, I guess, when I look back and do the math, were in their forties and fifties, taking care of us three bad kids. I feel like I had the best childhood, though.

I have so many good memories and don't remember lacking for anything. We didn't have a lot of money, though. We had a family home that my grandpa had pretty much paid off by the time he passed. It was a modest, 3-bedroom home. My grandparents had the front room and us kids shared the other two. At different points in my life, my mom or other aunts and uncles lived there as well, so they would take one of the rooms and us kids would all share a room at that point. We had mice, we had roaches, but the home was ours and everyone knew at any given point, they had a place to go that was home. In addition to his work paycheck, my grandfather also received a monthly retirement check from his time spent in the Navy. That was split between him and Rose, and she had her own separate check that she used however she so pleased. "Money is made to spend; you can't take it with you." That was Rose's philosophy on life, whereas my grandpa was the exact opposite. He was a saver and was always planning for a rainy day.

Their relationship dynamic always intrigued me, and the saying opposites attract couldn't be more true when it came to my grandparents' relationship. They had a ten-year age difference, with Rose being the older one. My grandma had been married before and she already had eight kids when she met my grandpa—Yeah, I know, right? Ha. They got married and had two kids together: my mom, Michelle, and the youngest, my Uncle Mack—or Wanky, as we called him. My grandma was a firecracker; very blunt and to the point, and she was not afraid to cuss you out, no matter who you were. With what I've already told you about my grandpa, you know that he was the exact opposite, so how they got together and made it work for so many years is beyond me. It's weird, because I can now see some parallels in my own marriage to how my grandparents were. My husband, Stephen, was also born on New Years' Day, just like Rose. They shared the same birthday. Stephen is also a spender—just like Rose. I'm the saver, like my grandpa. Crazy, right? I have also made my room my happy place and spend all my leisure time there, just like my grandpa used to.

Life wasn't perfect, but it was good. Growing up in the nineties, we had that sense of family that I grew to know and love. Things were going good from my perspective. I had never had to experience any major heartache or tragedy. That is, until Thursday, November 30, 2006.

Grandpa

LaChae

So even though it was more than fifteen years ago, I still
remember it like it was yesterday. I was in my second year of
college at IUP and Thanksgiving was the week before, so I had
literally just gotten back to school from being home on break.
Although my grandpa had a serious disposition to some, as I
was getting older, he had become so easy to talk to. Whenever I
was home, I enjoyed sitting in his room and just catching up on
things. We mainly talked about school and how those things
were going. We talked about the food at school and my
spending habits. I remember that clearly, because we had a
joint bank account that he was using to help support me
financially while I was in school. He would look at the statement
and he said to me, "You must not like the food at school since
you're always at Taco Bell." I always wonder if some people
have an idea that the end of their time on Earth is approaching.
When you reflect, you start to see they were giving you little

nuggets and pieces of information that were so much more meaningful after they passed.

In one of my last conversations with my grandfather and my mother, we talked about money management and saving. He showed us his bank statements and how much was in his savings account. I always saw my grandpa working so hard and honestly, when he shared his bank statement, it both shocked and inspired me. In no way was he a rich man, but he wasn't living paycheck to paycheck, either. He showed us how he had invested some of his money in a CD to make money off it, and as a young adult in college, he was really dropping gems, because these were things I never heard of. I knew my grandpa always had money when people asked to borrow it or when Rose got it into her mind that she wanted something, but I never knew his true financial situation.

My grandpa was smart with his money, and although he didn't do well in school, he was no dummy. He showed us the balance left on the mortgage and how if he wanted to, he could pay the house off, but he chose to prolong the payoff because if something were to happen to him, he didn't want my grandma Rose to worry about the taxes on the home. He thought it would be easier for her to just worry about the mortgage payments. He showed us his life insurance policy and how he paid the bare minimum on his extra policy because he said he didn't want to put too much in something that you hope won't happen. My grandpa also showed us how he had bought each of his grandkids— Me, Laurice, Reese, and Aren—a coin that he said he would gift to us at a later time. In the conversation, I didn't think he meant when he died, but that is exactly what happened. It was his last gift to us, and it had a special, handwritten message on the insert that said, "To my granddaughter, LaChae, may you never be broke, Love Granddad". That is probably one of the most precious gifts I have received in my life. I don't know if my siblings or my cousin were as impacted by the message, but that gift was my inspiration. I still have it to this day, and every now and then, when I need motivation, I find my coin and read the message in the insert. It is one of the reasons I push myself so hard to be successful because I always want to make him proud, and I wish he could see where I am and how much I've grown today.

But anyway, as you can see, it's kind of weird in hindsight that a week before his death, my grandpa shared all that information with us, right? It's something that always plagued my mind. But he was in good health, or so I thought. There was no sign, no indication that he was sick…nothing. I went back to school, and I remember I had started waking up early in the morning and walking for exercise to try to work off Thanksgiving and some of that Taco Bell I had been eating. My family had kept commenting on how I had gained weight on break, and I needed to try to work it off. It was about six in the morning, and I got a call from my mom's phone. I didn't think anything of it, and I answered as I was getting into the elevator to leave my 7th floor dorm to start my walk. I was cheerful as I answered, and I couldn't hear anything at first. I thought my mom was just surprised that I was up and active so early in the morning. Then, I heard it. She was crying and she couldn't form a sentence to get her words out. Instantly, I knew in my mind that something was wrong. At that time, I was nineteen and I hadn't really experienced much death in my life.

The first funeral I can fully remember attending was Aunt Delilah, and I believe she was my grandpa's aunt, but I don't know the exact relationship; I just know we called her Aunt Delilah. I didn't really know her that much; I just remember my grandpa taking us to visit her at her house on Emerald Street by the tax building. I was pretty young, and the only reason I went was because I had poison ivy, and I couldn't go to school. My siblings went to school that day and that is the only reason I was there. I remember my mom crying, but I didn't get it.

Then there was Uncle Wilbert. That was the first time I had seen Rose cry. We were sitting on the front porch of her house when she got a call and started crying and dropped the phone. The phone started ringing again and I answered it. Mind you, I was eleven, and I remember that happening in September, right around my birthday. When I answered it, there was a very official-sounding woman on the phone, and she repeated that she was informing the family of Wilbert Brown that he was deceased. Thinking back, I know I had to sound like a child. Why did the woman even tell me what was going on? He had died in jail, and they were informing us. Grandpa was a supportive husband, and we went down to Wallace funeral home. This was when they were in their old location that almost looked like a house in Steelton. I have seen them far too many times after that, because they then became our family funeral home that handled all the subsequent funerals. Grandpa went into the funeral home and paid for Uncle Wilbert's funeral in cash. Although Uncle Wilbert was close, my mom's brother, I still don't think I fully understood death. If I'm being completely honest, they sent us all my uncle's cool belongings and games and snacks, and I got to see all my family from Virginia. I didn't think about the fact that I lost my uncle, and I would never see him again.

But when I got that phone call that morning from my mom, it seemed final. I definitely understood what was going on. I remember trying to brace myself in my mind as my mom was stumbling over her words, trying to tell me what was going on…is it Rose or grandpa? I was in no way ready for it to be either one of them, but I just knew that something happened to one of my grandparents. It was agonizing, listening to my mom cry on the phone, and she never did tell me what was going on. She was so broken up that my cousin, Squirt, had to get on the phone and explain that my grandpa was gone. Just like that. How was that even possible? He wasn't sick and I had just left home. This death, I definitely understood, and it hit me like a ton of bricks. Somehow, we decided that I would go to my classes that day and leave to come home after that. That was pointless, because all of my teachers sounded like Charlie Brown's teachers. I remember being in my Microbiology class in a complete daze. I left school and drove home. I made it to Harrisburg in exactly two hours, even though IUP is three hours away.

My mom and Uncle Wanky were getting things together, but we had a pretty good idea of all the information we needed because grandpa had just shared everything with us. We had his funeral at Mount Zion and for a while after the funeral, whenever I went to church, all I could see in my mind was him lying in the casket. At first, I didn't get close to the casket. I saw him from the back and ended up leaving the church. It's crazy because as I was outside, I got a call from my cousins in the military, and I ended up leaving to show them how to get to the church. When I got back, I was finally able to make my way to the front. The strongest man I had ever met in my life up until that point was lifeless and stiff in a casket. I remember touching him and he felt cold, and I remember thinking, why does he have glasses on with his eyes closed? It was at that point it hit me; that was my grandpa's body only. It was no longer him. That was only a shell, and my grandpa wasn't in there. My great grandmother, his mother, cried the whole funeral. Her distinct cry stuck out in my mind. My brother didn't want to move from the casket. He seemed to have taken it the hardest. It wasn't until that point that I even thought about how he must have felt. He was the boy, the grandson that grandpa took under his wing. It must've really hurt him. He didn't really talk about it much, but his actions following grandpa's death showed that it really affected him.

That wasn't my first encounter with death, but it was the first one that I was old enough to understand, and it made a huge impact on my life. I still miss him and think about him to this day. I wish I could talk to him, and that he could see that I took all his advice and some of my own. I get satisfaction in knowing that I was able to do what he wanted me to do, and that was graduate from college and utilize my degree to break generational curses.

Background

Laurice

I know you heard my mom's and even my sister's point of view. Now, let me tell you my point of view. I am the middle child; very quiet, shy, and laid back. I am not one that is up for talking and expressing myself to others, but I knew I had a story to tell and what better way to do it than giving you all a glimpse on how things looked from my seat.

Growing up with my brother, Maurice Jr., and sister, LaChae, while living with our grandparents was not what most people or children would prefer, but it was all I knew, and so it was the norm for me. Although I had a lot of memorable moments and enjoyable times, I would be lying if I said I did not miss or want my parents, at times, to be together under the same roof. But, just as quick as the thought crossed my mind, it left.

My grandparents were like night and day—complete opposites of one another. How they met and stayed married for so many years is beyond me. My grandpa, also known as Mack, was very chilled and laid back. He did not say too much but when he did, you knew to sit back, listen, and take the advice he was giving, because ten times out of ten, he was always right. I admired my grandpa and knew that when I grew up, I had to have a man with the same qualities as him. He woke up every morning, put on his blue uniform, and went to work so that he could provide for his wife, kids, and grandkids, and I never once heard him complain. He would get off work, go up to his room, watch his television shows, and you could tell what he was watching by his responses. We would hear his yells travel down from the second floor. We would either hear him chuckling or shouting out all the correct answers from his Jeopardy shows.

Rose was the fiery firecracker; her mouth was lethal, and she was not to be played with. A lot of times, me and my siblings would fend for ourselves while Rose was down at the bar. I remember us being hungry, but not wanting to walk to the bar too early, because she would cuss us out and send us on our way. So, we had it mapped out; we would go when it was almost time for my grandpa to get off of work to hurry her up, because as I mentioned earlier, my grandpa was the bread winner and Rose took care of the house, and one thing that came with that was making sure he had a cooked meal every night. Even if it came burnt, with eggshells, or just no flavor, he would scarf it down like it was the best meal he had ever had. He knew how to keep the peace and he loved Rose unconditionally. My sister's memory is amazing, as you can see. She remembers every little detail. We often sit and talk, and she will tell me stories of something that happened when we were younger, and I just sit there smirking and intrigued, like, "Girl, you are lying." But what I do remember is that there was never a dull moment, and the fact that my aunts and uncles were always around was a plus.

Rose loved to drink, and some of her kids did too, so they would gather a few times a week, come over, drink, play cards, and call me into the kitchen to dance for them as their entertainment. I remember hearing, "Go, Laurice, Go, Laurice, get it girl!" That is when I would really show out. Now that I am grown, I don't have to hide that secret, knowing I cannot get in trouble by my mom. When the adults were not looking, I would drink the little drops that were left in their beer cans. I would see my sister, LaChae, out of the corner of my eye, smirking and shaking her head. I always made sure that Reece was nowhere in sight, because he would have dimed me out, for sure. Once I was done, I would go back to the dance floor, also known as Rose's kitchen, and begin to dance some more, hearing, "Go, Laurice, get it girl." The night typically ended with someone getting cussed out by Rose. Then, she would go upstairs and lay next to my grandpa and go to sleep comfortably, like she didn't just cuss everyone out and tell them to get out of her house. My grandpa would never say anything; he would fall asleep as well and they both would wake up like nothing ever happened. There was never a dull moment in our house, and my family dynamic was crazy. We laughed, fought, and cried together. We did not have a traditional household with a mom and dad, but we had grandparents that made sure that we were loved and cared for, and they were the glue that held our family together. That is, until November 30, 2006, when our lives changed dramatically.

Grandpop

Laurice

Waking up in a daze, frazzled, and confused were the emotions that instantly came across my body. I could see three figures in my room, so I quickly adjusted my vision to get a better look. I turned to my little brother who was sitting on my bed, halfway awake, looking to me for answers as to why he was being awakened so early on a school day. Little did he know, I was just as confused as he was. I then turned to my cousin Squirt, and I thought to myself, "This is weird." She has two kids that she needs to get ready for school and plus, she has never come to our house this early in the morning. As I looked into her eyes, I instantly knew something was wrong, so I then turned to my mom for answers, and I could see tears running down her eyes as she uttered, "Grandpop is gone." I instantly froze, my stomach dropped, and I wished God would allow me to just say one last thing to him. My mind was spinning. I was thinking about everything that I wanted to say, needed to say, hoped to say, but just could not say.

We all had our own little things we would do to spend personal time with him. LaChae, being the outspoken, older sister, she would always go sit on the bed next to him and just buss it up and talk to him. It did not matter what it was about; school, everyday life, anything. But it felt like they would be up there speaking for hours, and I would just sit in the background, thinking how boring their conversations were. I can now say I appreciate the times she took to gain knowledge from him, because now she is my go-to. Anything that has happened or is happening in my life, I go to my sister. She is a very smart, open-minded individual. She tends to tell everyone she is the Beyonce of the family, but she is that plus more, and I could not ask for a better role model than her.

Now, Reece, being the only boy in the house, he often felt outnumbered and would always go to my grandpop complaining about us. But they had their little man time too. My grandpop played his numbers faithfully at the Beer Distributor around the corner from the house. When he would get off work, he would come home, get Reece, and they would go play his numbers. The people at the Beer Distributor knew the both of them by name in the store and knew the exact time each day to expect them to come through those doors. Once they would return home, Reece would come through the door with a sneaky smile and a lollipop. He knew to follow my grandpop up the steps to eat his lollipop in peace, because me, being his annoying, older sister, I more than likely would have snatched it and ran. Yes, you know I am one of Michelle's kids.

My relationship with my grandpa was very unique. I loved being around him. We did not say too much, but our presence from being around one another spoke volumes. Although I did not speak much, I would come and lay in the bed with my grandpa while he watched TV. I remember helping to assist him in his man-made garden, and even sat with him in his shed while he worked on one of his many projects. My grandpa was a very smart, wise man. I would oftentimes go to him whenever I had a big project that was due and after working long hours, he would still manage to set some time for us to work on my projects daily, until it was completed.

As I began to get older, I would ask him to help me with every project that came about, because if you knew my grandpa, you knew he would get excited and get carried away by doing the assignment on his own. I did not care that the projects did not look like a kid did the work, I was just happy that I did not have to do it myself. I started to realize that my grandpa loved and enjoyed being able to be our go-to person and feeling needed. I also realized that I never really needed help, I just enjoyed going to my grandpa so that we could have our one-on-one time together, because everyone else had their own things going on with him.

All those memories crossed my mind as I sat on my bed in disbelief. I could not believe our family was falling apart. This was the first time I had actually experienced death so close to home. I knew people eventually passed at some point, but I do not think I fully understood the concept of death. I remember slowly walking to my grandpop's casket, heart beating and mind racing a mile a minute. I remember being so anxious but yet, nervous at the same time. I was so scared to touch his body, but I felt like I could not be scared this time, as I was scared to talk to him as a child. I remember telling myself I had to be brave because I would never get another chance. I quickly rubbed my fingers across his face and whispered my last goodbye.

Every child has that one superhero that they look up to and admire. Well, mine was my grandpa. I admired the fact that he stepped in for me and acted like my father when he did not have to. If you ask anyone, my grandparents would let it be known that we were their kids. My grandpa may have physically left this

Earth on that day, but he left behind a lot of wisdom that he instilled in every last one of us, and I will forever be grateful.

My Mother is My Oldest Daughter

Michelle

As I reflect, I can see my mother had Alzheimer's and Dementia early on, but because we didn't know the signs and symptoms, it went undetected. Before my father passed, my mother had another heart attack. I remember going down to the bar that my mother would patronize often and asking to speak to the owner of the bar. I noticed while I was standing in the bar, they had a list of names of people that were banned from the bar. As I waited, I knew several people from high school that were in the bar. They were asking me what I was doing in the bar, and I had to let them know I was waiting on Mr. Odes, the owner. My mother would often talk about me being saved. She would not say saved, though; she would tell people that I was in the church now. I believe that made my mother happy, and she did not have to worry about me as much. She saw a difference in me. While I was standing there, waiting on Mr. Odes, a guy came from the floor of the bar and asked me to follow him down in the bottom, underneath the floor of the bar. I was amazed at what I saw when I went down there. I had no Idea of what was in the floor of the bar. A real, live, Man Cave. However, I knew what I was there for, and I had to go into the enemy's camp to help save my mother.

My mother was the pistol and the bullet, all in one. If she knew I was there, and what I was about to do and say, what I was going to say to the owner of the bar, she would be truly angry with me and would cuss me out. But my mother's life was on the line, and I was not about to allow it to go down like that. I began to tell Mr. Odes that my mother was sick and not allowed to drink anymore, and I did not want to see my mother in his place of establishment anymore. I told Mr. Odes if I found out my mother was in there and she got sick again, that I was going to hold him liable. When I walked out of the bar that day, my mother's name had been added to the banned list, which allowed the bartenders to know that my mom was not allowed to be in there ever again. If she showed up, she was to be asked to leave. I did not know then, but I know now, that put me on the enemy's hit list. My mother should have been snatched out of here in the late nineties, before the passing of my father.

Being that my mother was not allowed to go to the bar any longer, she would have what she wanted delivered to her house. She used home delivery—Door Dash, before Door Dash existed. She found another way, along with my siblings, Tony and Joyce, who would get her what she wanted. Every day after the passing of my father, I would go over to my parents' house to check on my mother and make sure she was okay, and to see what she needed before I would go home for the evening. One evening, I stopped by and my two brothers, my sister, and my niece were all in the house, and my mom was drinking. I got angry at my siblings and could not believe they were all sitting around, allowing my mother to drink. Everyone in the house knew I was angry. My sister, Joyce, made a comment to me, "Your dad is dead, get over it." Get over it, and I just lost my father, is she serious right now? I lost it. My niece told me that they had a bet that me being saved was just a game and this was a phase that I was going through. Was I hearing all of this? My feelings were hurt. Was my family trying to push the knife in a little further to my heart? My family thought that I was playing with God. Little did they know that God had gotten ahold of me, and I was never going back into the world. He chose me and called me to come on out of the world.

It was not until my mother's stay in the hospital after Mother's Day that God set it up so that I could move my mother in with me. She would never go back to my parents' house again. A nursing home was not an option. Before bringing my mother home, we had a family discussion and what we all decided was best was that my mother would move in with me, and my siblings, along with her grandchildren, would help care for her. I did not know then that the next ten years would be a journey. I would be taking care of my mother, who would become my oldest daughter. I had to sit back and watch this woman, who was strong willed and very vocal, revert back to a child. I saw how fragile life looked through my mother. I would wonder why God would allow the roles to be reversed. There were days that I would come home from work after my older sister and brother would come by and give my mother things that she was not allowed to have. They would leave the house, leaving me to clean up the mess or deal with my mother's attitude.

I will never forget coming home after one long day at work. My sister had stopped by that day, and she gave my mother chocolate milk, which was something that upset my mother's stomach. My sister had left the house right before I arrived home. I went through the door and when I tell you that my cream carpet was horrible, I mean horrible. All I could do was sit in the middle of the floor and cry and cry, asking God what was going on. I needed God to help me and give me the grace, strength, and patience to be able to care for my mother with love and do it to the best of my abilities.

Months after my mom moved in, I began to really see the changes in her. The family who said they would be there were not coming around on a regular basis. It ended up being my younger brother, Mack Jr., and my children, LaChae, Laurice, and Maurice Jr., who would help take care of my mother, along with my sister-neighbor, Sharon. God put a support system in place. I eventually realized that this was my assignment, and not anyone else's. God gave me grace and strategies throughout the years. I cannot tell you how I did it, only that it was the grace of God. When I could no longer move my mother, God gave me the idea to put my mother into her wheelchair and push her to the bathroom to bathe her. My place of employment gave me favor, along with FMLA, to take care of my mother. My brother's place of employment allowed him to work from home. I knew that was only God's favor. During the day, my younger brother would take care of my mother. I would dress my mother, get her food ready in the morning, and then go to work with a smile on my face. I would pray and cry some days, all the way to work. My prayer was, "Lord, once I arrive inside this building, please put a smile on my face. No one needs to know what I am going through. Let me not take my personal life into my place of employment." I was grateful that my younger brother moved here to help me take care of our mother. God put things in place the entire time for us.

I finally put my foot down and I would not allow my other siblings, Tony and Joyce, to come to the house after a certain time, because they would come by to wake my mother up, get her upset, and then leave within five to ten minutes, and then I had to deal with her the rest of the night.

I would give my mother money, like you would do a child, because that was something that she was used to having. But eventually, I had to stop doing that because all my mom would do is give it away. See, no matter what state of mind my mother was in, one of the things she would do was always give her money away to her children, and them boys could get anything from my mom. Once I began to put my foot down and give house rules, my family would turn their back on my mom and stop speaking to me and stop coming around. "How could they do this to my mother?" I would ask myself.

My mother and my niece, Squirt, had a closer relationship than my mother and I did, and she was no longer coming around with her family to visit my mother. This hurt; this was the same niece I grew up with, and my mother raised us together like sisters. My niece was like my sister, and we were only a few months apart. I took her advice, and then she stopped speaking to me. I did not know what I did wrong. For a few years, it bothered me. I tried to reach out to her, but she would not respond. I had to tell God to work on me and my heart. Family hurt, but I had to go on, because I had a mother who needed me.

I will say, when it was time for my mother to go to her doctor appointments, someway, somehow, the siblings and the grandchildren would all come together to take my mother in the early years. This would put a smile on my mother's face. She would talk about the old times and my father. I really believe that after my father passed, my mother was not the same. She appeared motionless. My mother would often tell me she missed my dad. Even when she was not able to remember names, she remembered that she was married, and she had a husband. My oldest daughter, LaChae, would have a look on her face at times when my mother did not remember who she was, because she would tell everyone that she was the favorite of all. My mother had ten kids, twenty grands, and several great-grands. My son, Maurice Jr., was the one that kept her laughing, and my baby brother was her baby, even though he was thirty-something. The doctors would tell us that we were doing an excellent job with my mother. Her health was much better, and things had turned around. Her only problem was that she did not remember at times, and she wasn't able to get around that well.

I really got to know my mother on an entirely different level by taking care of her and listening to her stories. I did not realize how strong my mother was, and that she did the best she could do growing up. My mother was raised by her grandmother, because her mother had passed away when she was a young girl. Her father did what he knew to do too, so he had help from his mother to raise my mother and her twin brother. My mother loved to sing and dance, and as a little girl, she would get beat for dancing and singing. My mother had her first child at the age of thirteen and was married three times. My mother never had the opportunity to be a child, and she did not know how to be a mother, so she did the best that she could do. My mom showed her love by buying us things. She would always say, "Money is made to spend."

One thing for sure is she loved kids, and she helped raise several of my nieces and nephews until they reached a certain age, when she would send them home to be with their parents.

My parents did an excellent job helping me with my children. My children never missed a beat. My parents loved my children. My mother would often tell me that I just had the kids, but they were hers. My mom meant every word of it, too. I remember one time when I went to her house to pick my children up, and she told me that they were not going anywhere, and she tried to throw hot water on me. My parents enjoyed my children's company, so there were times I would allow my children to just stay with them. Also, my mother had a way with words that would cut you. Now that my mother had Alzheimer's and Dementia, I got to dress her up, comb her hair, and do things she would not normally let me do. I loved my oldest daughter—my mother.

I remember one day, I was going out on a date with my second husband and no matter where we went, he would be upset because I would always be late. He did not know what I had to do to get out of the house to go out. It was not that easy for me. I remember the doctors put my mother on a medication that they said would help with the Alzheimer's, and I am here to tell you that it did the total opposite. My mother started hallucinating, saying that she wanted to kill herself. She would go up and down the stairs, screaming and hollering. She did not sleep that night, and I was nervous. After the first night and the first dose, I threw the medicine away and I told the doctor what had happened. He did not seem surprised at all. All I knew was my mother was not going to take that medicine that only made things worse. Back to my ex-husband, who I was dating at the time; we all decided to go to my cousin's house for a family gathering one year, and it was not until then that he saw how I took care of my mother and what being her caregiver entailed. Then and right then, he finally understood why I was always late to the dates.

On November 30, 2009, he came to my house in the morning, before my son went to school, and we went into the room with my mother, where he asked me to marry him. He knew that day was a sad day, so he wanted to put a smile on my face. My mother did not understand what was going on, and I found out after the marriage ended that my children did not like my ex-husband, but they did not want to say anything because they wanted me to be happy. Taking care of my mother required putting my life on hold to make sure she had the best care possible.

I thank God, because God gave me the grace to do what needed to be done. I look back and realize that it was all God. There were times that I would arrive to church late, but I would just say to myself, "I am here." No one knew the struggles I was going through on the inside and the conversations I would have with myself. It was a sacrifice, at times, just to get myself dressed and to go to church. Going to church and work was my outlet. That is how I was able to cope and get through another week, another month, and even another year. When others were traveling and talking about what they did over the weekend, I was home. I went in the house on a Thursday or a Friday, and I did not come back out unless I was going to church on Sunday or work on Monday.

I remember one of the sisters that I went to church with did a radio broadcast called *Showers of Blessings with Sharon*. It was a Saturday morning, and I did not want to be late to the radio station as we only had one hour. I had to make sure my mother was good, that was not an option, but it was either be late or wrinkle. So, I left the house wrinkled that morning, something that I would not normally do. This sister in Christ asked me why I would leave the house looking like that. I guess I looked a mess. I said to myself, "If she only knew." She knew I took care of my mother, how could she say that? But from that day on, I made sure I was not wrinkled again. However, the struggle was real at times. Being a caregiver was not an easy job, but I will say it was rewarding, especially knowing that my mother lived longer than she was expected to just by coming under my roof.

While my mother was able to still talk, I was able to lead her to Christ. I remember asking her if she wanted to be saved, and she told me, "Yes." No matter what happened, I knew my mother was going to Heaven. That is why I knew it was my assignment that my mother had to come stay with me. The sleepless nights, the frustration, the mess I would come home to, the tears I had to cry, putting my life on hold, the things I had to let go of; it was worth it all to have my mother saved.

My mother was hospitalized and had another stroke, but she recovered. Being my mother's caregiver, I began to learn my mother, and I could tell when she was not feeling well or was not herself. As I mentioned in a previous chapter, it appears that when I am doing something for the Kingdom, something seems to happen. But what it let me know also, as I began to write this book, is that hell must be angry at me, and I never knew until now what I possess on the inside of me.

November 2016, and I just so happened to join a 30-day prayer call with Bishop John Guns. Here we go again, Wednesday, November 30, 2016. I joined the prayer call that morning, and a little later I went into my mother's room. I noticed that she was having a stroke. I called the ambulance, and they rushed her to the hospital. She did not look good. After all the tests were ran, the doctors said that she arrived too late to the hospital, so they could not give her anything to reverse the stroke. They told me if my mother would eat anything, she might choke. I said to the doctors, "Okay, what do we do now? Where do we go from here?" He told me that it was time to call in hospice. With my mother not being able to eat, there was nothing else they could do. They asked if I wanted my mother to go to the hospice facility or keep her in the hospital. I told them that my mother was going home with me. I could see the look in my mother's eyes and the tear that ran down her face. I knew she could hear us but was unable to respond. My mother could not talk or eat as a result to this last stroke. Lord, what was I going to do? My oldest daughter, my mother, was leaving me.

Being my mother's caregiver helped me to love, forgive, have patience, and showed me—more of me. My mother helped fill the void left by Maurice Jr. I was so busy taking care of my mother that I did not completely grieve the loss of my son. I would be lost without her. My routine would be interrupted. We had grown so close. Why God? Why now? I took my mother home with instructions, cleared my living room out for a hospital bed, and a nurse showed up to show me how to administer medicine for the pain. Hospice asked a series of questions: if I wanted a nurse to come in to relieve me, did I want someone to play a violin for me, or did I need a chaplain to come pray with me. I said, "No," to everything. All I wanted was to be left alone. I could not believe my mother was going to pass in my presence. All I could do was think about when my father took his last breath. I just sat with my mother, prayed with my mother, and played music for my mother. I gave my mother popsicles to keep her mouth moistened. My mom just gave me a stare that I will never forget. The nurse would come out each day, not knowing that they told me that they did not think that my mom would live another day, or even through the weekend. But we know it is not over until God says it is over.

It was Monday, December 5, 2016; Day five of the 30-day prayer call. The hospice nurse called to say she would be coming to visit my mother in an hour. I remember over the weekend having a conversation with my mother, and I told her it was okay for her to go. I would be okay. I knew my mother did not want to see me alone. She wanted to see me with someone and happy. She would often say to me, "When are you going to get married? Why don't you have a husband?" I sat with my mom that morning, cleaned her up, and had her looking good. The nurse looked at me and told me to call the family to come say their goodbyes, because my mom would be leaving us soon. I called my girls, LaChae and Laurice, and I got my baby brother, Mack Jr., on the phone. I do not know how my girls arrived at my house so quickly. I remember it like it was yesterday. I had this old, ugly t-shirt on, and I had not bathed yet. I am quite sure I smelt horrible. My brother was on the phone, and we were there, and she left us.

My niece arrived, and my neighbor came over. The hospice nurse held me tight as I cried in her arms. My mom, Rose, my oldest daughter, took her last breath. I was looking around and before I knew it, the undertaker had arrived. I remember the nurse taking all the medication, but I do not remember when or who took the hospital bed. I had cleared my living room out to make room for the hospital bed, so I had no furniture to sit on. The only thing I wanted to do was go crawl in my bed. Another crack to my heart, yet again. The day before my grandson's birthday. I was in no mood for anything. I had to trust God through this process again.

November and December's memories are ones that I would never forget, but I needed God to help me live through them and help me to heal. Anyone who still has their parent should love and cherish them. It is more of a joy than a burden to be able to take care of the person that raised you when God turns the table and reverses the raising. I learned that there is purpose in everything we do. Being my mother's caregiver was more for me than it was for her. It helped me and made me grow up even more.

There came a time when I had to allow my younger brother to go live his life. Through all this, my baby brother, Mack Jr., had been diagnosed with bone cancer. Lord knows I was trying to keep it all together; Going to his doctor appointments, chemo, radiation, making sure his room was clean. It felt like I had the world on my shoulders, trying to make sure both Mack Jr. and my mom were good.

I had to come to the decision that it was time to allow Mack Jr. to go live life, and I would be okay taking care of our mother. Mack Jr. reminded me so much of my father; he was very quiet and mild mannered. Through his own health issues, he was right there, helping with our mother. He never complained; you would have never known what he was going through because he never showed it, nor did he let his own health issues stop him. He smiled through it. He worked and took care of our mother without missing a beat. My brother told me what was so sad was seeing the children that were diagnosed with cancer. That hurt his heart. I could not be selfish; it was time I told my brother that he should move to a warmer climate because it would be better for his health. I knew in my heart that he did not want to go, but he would do whatever I would ask him to do. I knew he respected me and trusted my decisions. We had several conversations about his health and what would be best.

I am glad that he decided to move to Florida, because it was October 8, 2020, when I received a call from my uncle while I was at work, telling me that Mack Jr. passed away from a heart attack. I remember being in my office, falling to the floor, and screaming, "No, not Wankey! No, this cannot be, my baby brother!" My brother was like my twin; my best friend. We talked about everything, just like I did with our father. My baby brother was like my older son. Yes, another tear in my heart. I love all my siblings and I miss all of them that have passed on. It is just that Mack Jr. and I grew up together, so we had a different type of bond. I was his big sister that he looked up to. There were many days that I had to depend on God. I saw Him answer prayers and turn things around. I learned to call on God for myself. My mother had three heart attacks and three strokes, and God kept her living when we thought she would go before my father. No one knows the plan of God. If I had to do it all over again, my answer would still be YES: Yield Everything and Surrender. I often wonder what my oldest daughter, who is my mother, would be doing today if she was still here. I miss my mom!! I learned a lot from you!

A Rose is Still a Rose

LaChae

Have you ever met someone that made you feel special? Like y'all had a special bond that was only shared between the two of you? Then, you later find out that same person you thought you had a bond with made everybody feel that way? That is the best way to explain my grandma Rose. She would do things for you, like slide you a couple dollars when no one else was watching, and then tell you not to tell anyone. She would make you feel like there was this inside secret that no one else knew, and the whole time, as soon as you walked away, she was sliding my brother or my aunt a couple dollars and telling them the same thing. For as long as I can remember, Rose was there. From what I've been told, I'm the only one of her many grandkids that she was able to see be born. So, of course, I thought I was special. I would even go as far as to say I was her favorite. She called me Shay-de-bird—don't even get me to lying about how you even spell that. The way I would describe Rose is the most unaffectionate person I know. Unless she had a few, she never told you she loved you, didn't hug or kiss, or anything like that. Most of the time, she was fussing at you more than anything, and if you didn't really know her, you might think she was mean. But the thing with Rose was she never had to tell you she loved you; you just knew.

If I had to guess, I would say she expressed love in what she did for others, which was her love language. She would always do something nice, like buy your favorite snack at the store, cook your favorite food, or, like I mentioned before, make my grandpa's coffee every morning. She didn't bite her tongue and just as quick as she could make you feel special, she could also hurt your feelings and make you cry. She helped me have thick skin. It was not uncommon that if you started gaining weight, Rose would tell you, "You're getting as big as a house." From the time I was little, I was always with Rose, and she used to take me everywhere. Rose never drove, so she would catch a city bus in a heartbeat. I loved when she would let me put the change in the machine. Back in the day, we used to have to pay an extra 35 cents for a transfer. She had me everywhere. I remember one time, we were uptown on 6th Street. We had caught the bus up there. I was very little at the time and Rose was distracted by me when someone snatched her bag and ran off. Rose yelled after him and tried to run to get it back, but I was there and I remember I started crying, so the guy got away. I don't know if this incident had anything to do with it, but Rose would then carry her money in a sock that she stuffed in her bra. I guess she figured nobody could get to her money that way. It used to be so embarrassing, going to the store with her. She would dig in her bra and pull out the sock. Most of the time, it was one of my grandpa's black dress socks. She would keep balled up bills and change in that sock. And she would stand in line at the store and count out money from the sock to pay for her stuff.

In one of our adventures on the bus, I got a bit curious. I had watched Rose put her wig on before we left. It fascinated me that the wig came on and off, and I pulled the wig off on the bus, in front of everybody. Rose was so embarrassed. She cussed me out the whole way home.

One thing about Rose, she was never too proud, and she loved free stuff. She would take me and my siblings to, "the church to eat." I don't know how she knew when and where all the soup kitchens were, but we would wait in line and be let in for lunch. Volunteers would serve us our meals and we would get juice that was so nasty. It tasted like they sweetened it with Sweet 'n Low. We sat there and ate with the homeless and less fortunate people and left and went back home where there was plenty of food. Rose just used her resources to get us all a free meal. When I was younger, that was when we ate out. All the other meals Rose cooked at home. Have you ever seen your grandma make tacos? Not me. She would cook full meals and have them ready when my grandpa came home from work. Rose also wasn't a stranger to going to food banks and getting free food to cook those meals. Rose didn't work. She was a stay-at-home housewife, and she made it work by any means necessary.

To this day, I'm still confused about her history. She always told us certain stories, like how she had a twin brother and a sister that lived in New York. That was true. How she had a metal plate in her head and that's why she would sometimes have headaches… I think we figured out that wasn't true as she got older and we started going to the doctors with her. Her mom was a white woman that died when she was very young, so she was raised by her dad. Well, she later changed her story a little bit and said her mom spoke Spanish. Which, honestly, hey, maybe back in those days, she considered her white and my grandma's name was Rosa…things that make you go, "Hmmm." So, needless to say, I don't know how many of the stories she told were actually true. Even more so when she developed dementia—she could definitely put a story together.

When Rose started to noticeably lose her memory and, sometimes, even her sense of reality, I was away at college. After my grandpa passed, I think Rose went into a bit of depression, even though she would never speak those words. She stayed in her house for a while by herself. When I would call home, I would start to hear stories about how Rose was making up things and telling stories to people, but I wasn't there to witness it for myself, so I laughed it off and didn't believe any of them.

My grandma was friends with Ms. Mary, one of my roommate's grandmas. Rose told me that Ms. Mary was dating a midget, and she was too embarrassed to tell anybody, so she was keeping it a secret. Listen, before you go judging me, this was the grandma that was a straight shooter, *tell it like it is*, all my life. She had never lied to me about anything before, so I believed it. And what did I do? I told my roommate! Now looking back, all I can do is laugh, because I believed my grandma and I was so serious when I told this girl that her grandma was dating a midget. So, what did she do? She went back and asked her grandma! This is a real-life story; I cannot make this up... but apparently, Rose could. She was lying and Ms. Mary cussed her granddaughter out for even asking her such a thing. Hindsight is

20/20, and Rose went through this phase where she would not miss a Jerry Springer episode, so she was most likely mixing up reality with what she was watching on the show. Even then, I still thought it was funny and didn't see anything wrong with what Rose was doing, until she got me.

So, I remember coming home for Christmas break. We had a good Christmas and Rose came over my mom's to celebrate with us. As it got later into the evening, I had plans to go out bowling with my friends, and I was asked to drop Rose off before I went about my way, so I did. Nothing eventful happened; I dropped her off at home and went out. Don't you know when I came home, my mom and Uncle Wanky had an attitude with me. My mom said, "You were in that much of a rush that you were speeding in the car with your grandma and got pulled over?" The whole time, I was looking at them like they were crazy, because what were they taking about? Rose had done told them that I was speeding when taking her home and the cops pulled me over and said they were going to let me go because it was Christmas, and I had my granny in the car. Ya'll, she imagined that whole scenario in her head, because it never happened. I stopped taking up for her and believing her stories from that point forward.

It was hard watching someone that I had so much love and respect for essentially revert back into a child-like state. I didn't really understand dementia, and I always felt bothered the most because it almost seemed like because I wasn't around when it started, she always forgot who I was. She would remember everyone else in the household, but sometimes struggled and ask me if I was my uncle's girlfriend. It wasn't all the time, but I remember feeling like saying, "Stop playing, you know me, snap out of it!" On some days, she was good and could tell you everything and act like you were tripping for treating her like she didn't know anything, but there were other days when she legitimately could not tell me my name or recognize me as someone that was familiar to her.

When Rose got to the point where she was wearing depends and hiding them around the house like a kid that wet the bed on themselves and didn't want their mom to find out, I knew she wasn't the same and we had to adjust to the new normal for her. She went from walking with a cane to needing a walker. Sometimes you would come in and see her scooting or crawling, getting into stuff she knew she had no business being in. It was like the roles reversed, and she was the child, while my mom was the parent. But one thing Rose never lost was that slick mouth of hers. She had some moments when she was really nice and sweet, but if you didn't let her have her way, she would still cuss you out—dementia and all.

When Rose took a turn for the worse from a final stroke, it was a difficult time. Hospice had been called in to educate and prepare us for her last days. They gave us these pamphlets and told us everything we were going to see and what to look out for. Rose got set up in a hospital bed in the living room. I listened and I asked questions, but the whole time I was thinking, "How do they know what's going to happen? How do they know how she's feeling?" None of them had died before, so I was listening but still kind of holding off hope that they were wrong. Rose had multiple strokes before, and she had pulled through, so I was thinking that she was somehow going to make it through that one as well. But this one was different; she wasn't able to even talk after this one. Her eyes were wide open, and she was looking at us like she was signaling or communicating through her eyes, but she couldn't speak because of how the stroke had affected her. They even told us that we couldn't feed her anything because she could end up aspirating and getting it into her lungs. Basically, we just needed to make her comfortable. We must've all been on the same page thinking, "How can she be comfortable not being able to eat or drink anything for days?" The hospice people said that she wasn't hungry, and you lose those feelings when transitioning, but again, she couldn't talk, so how would they know?

My mom is so hard-headed and wasn't letting her mom go out like that, so she started feeding Rose popsicles. She seemed to enjoy them too. Those people didn't know what they were talking about. That's what was still in my head. This went on for a few days; I don't really remember how long. I was still going to work and checking in after work, and on December 5th, I had the day off. I got dressed and went to my mom's, and Rose was different then; no more pleading with her eyes, her eyes were closed, and she had very labored breathing. My mom was there and the lady from hospice was there, and they knew what was up, I guess, but I still wasn't even thinking that day was about to be the day. Not even an hour after I got there, they told us it was about to happen, and we watched Rose take her last breaths. I honestly didn't even know that she had transitioned, and my mom even asked the lady from hospice for confirmation, and she confirmed she was gone. It gave me a little bit of peace by being there though, because she went so peacefully, and I knew she was no longer suffering.

Rose

Laurice

So, by now, I am pretty sure you have a good picture as to who and what Rose was like. My sister and I often joke with my mom by telling her, "Rose would *NEVER*." There was nothing in this world that Rose would not do for her grandkids. Now, you think Madea was a mess, but I tell you, she does not have anything on Rosa E. Thrasher. From carrying knives in her purse and her linty sock that she kept tied up and stored in her bra. I used to be appalled that she would walk around with one boob lumpy due to the sock in her bra, but Rose did not care. To cussing the kids out at the bus stop for picking on us, and telling them to go get their moms, dads, and grandmas—she was ready for whoever. It is funny because every time I have a chance to catch up with my dad, he tells me the same story about Rose waiting at the door with a .45 pistol, telling him he better not come any closer, not even caring what her daughter, my mom, had just done a few minutes prior to him coming to the house.

He realized that he was not going to get through to Rose, so he then proceeded to speak to my grandpa—the calmer parent that was not threatening him with a pistol.

Although my grandma battled an alcohol addiction, she still loved us, and we loved her more than words could explain. I never told her, but I felt as though I had to watch after my grandmom, to protect her. I remember many nights that I would stay up, looking out of the window, waiting patiently for her to come walking down Sycamore Street from her normal spot, Cloverly Heights. There may have been a few times I would look out the window to check to see if I could see my grandma and I would see her bent over across the street, unable to move. Feeling as though I was her protector, her savior, I would race across the street to be with her until she was finally able to stand her body straight up, and we would walk across the street to the house. She would go lay next to my grandpa and I would eventually go to bed, when I knew she was settled in. Rose was the definition of a strong, determined woman. When she had her mind set on something, she had to achieve it and could not wait on anyone. Rose would have us mowing the grass, carrying dressers out of the house, we did it all. I appreciate her for teaching me that I am able to do anything a man is capable of doing. I can probably count on one hand how many times I saw her show any emotions. Sometimes, I used to think that she was just a tough cookie. I remember sitting in her kitchen one day with my brother, sitting close to the refrigerator. She went to open the refrigerator and the glass bowl that was on top fell onto my brother's head, leaving a deep gash. I have never seen Rose be so hurt or have so much empathy as she did that day. She loved her grandson and the fact that she did something, on accident, to cause him pain, caused her pain.

The very next time I saw my grandma show emotion was when she received the call that her son, my uncle Wilbert, had passed away. We were sitting on the porch one summer day, and Rose had gone into the kitchen to get her some ice water from her icemaker. I remember thinking to myself, "Rose has been in the house for a minute, maybe she got distracted and started doing something around the house?" Not two seconds later, we heard a loud screech and someone crying out for help. I will never forget the sound of a mother crying out for her child and asking God, "Why?" To receive notification over the phone that your child has passed away. I just stared at my grandma, who was laying on the floor with the phone off the hook, siting right beside her. At the time, I did not know what to do as a child to console her. All I ever knew and saw was my grandma being strong, and not really showing too many emotions. I did not know how she felt, but I knew these were probably the same feelings and emotions my mom felt on the evening of November 19, 2014.

My Miracle Man

Michelle

I will jump all over the place and then I will pick back up and get you to the end. I called Maurice Jr. my Miracle Man, because he came into this world unexpectedly, and he left this world unexpectedly. I worked at Polyclinic Hospital at the time. I knew several of the doctors there. I started out in Dietary, and I went to school to be a medical assistant and I ended up working on Labor and Delivery. Dr. Ayodeji Olumuyiwa Bakare, MD - Harrisburg, PA, had delivered Laurice, who I thought would be my last child. I said I wanted two children, and I was done. Carrying Laurice, they told me that my baby was a boy. I bought all boy clothes; every baby shower gift was something for a little boy. Wouldn't you know it, the doctors had that one wrong. It was a girl. How could they get this wrong on the ultrasound? I did not get my boy then, and little did I know, God had another plan.

I remember being at work, not feeling well, and I told Dr. Bakare how I was feeling. He told me to make an appointment to see him. Not thinking anything of it, I did just that. Pregnancy was the furthest thing from my mind, since Dr. Bakare performed a tubal ligation on me March 12, 1990—the day after I gave birth to Laurice. Cut, tied, and burned everything. I refused to leave the hospital until it was done. I knew my family was very fruitful and multiplied, so I wanted to limit my fruit. However, I showed up to my appointment with my friend, Carmen. Dr. Bakare did an ultrasound and he told me to get dressed and come into his office to talk. The news I received was that I was pregnant. "What are you saying to me? I had my tubes cut, tied, and burned, how could this be?" I asked. He went on to tell me that the procedure is only 99% guaranteed and I just happen to be in that 1%. My nose began to bleed right in his office. I remember him telling me it was going to be okay; he was going to send me for another ultrasound to see how far along I was. I asked, "How can I be pregnant? I am still having a menstrual cycle, my tubes are tied and burned, what is going on here? Am I being punked, or what?"

I was five months pregnant and if I kept my baby, the baby would be due in November of 1993. It was already late July or early August, and within the next ninety days, I would give birth to Maurice Geter Jr. on November 15,1993.

Six months after giving birth to my Miracle Man, I found out that my first ex-husband had a child by someone else who was 10-18 months old. I remember Kathy and I walking through the hospital, going to visit a friend, and while we were having a conversation, I told her I knew. We were talking about two different things. She thought I meant I knew Maurice Sr. had another child. That day, I found out he had a baby, and no one wanted me to know because they wanted me to be happy; no one wanted to hurt me. Everyone was keeping this secret from me, or they thought I knew and was just putting up with his mess. They did not know what was actually going on behind closed doors. Yes, I was devastated, but it was also my way of escape from a toxic marriage and an abusive husband. I looked forward and never looked back. Maurice Sr. wanted this child; he did everything in his power to make sure that I was okay, and the baby was fine. While I was carrying our child, he knew it was a possibility that another woman had given birth to a child that turned out to be his.

My Miracle Man would be snatched from me twenty-one years later. My question to God was, "Why would You allow me to conceive and carry a child, my baby child, my only son? Why did my son have to be murdered?" Maurice Jr. was so full of life and energy, with big dreams and a big heart. I would always tell Maurice Jr., "The sky is the limit; all things are possible if you put God first." As a child, Maurice was like a sponge; he would absorb and memorize books. At the age of three, Maurice Jr. would read me his books that my mom would read to him every day. One day, I opened the book backwards and he read the book from the beginning to the end. That is when I realized that my baby had a memory like an elephant; he could not read, he just memorized the pages.

The Maurice I loved and raised would help anyone who had a problem. He would always bring home people that were in trouble and needed a place to stay. Maurice looked out for the underdog. If your son ran away from home and he was a friend of Moe's, nine times out of ten, he was at our house hiding in Maurice's room. That was Maurice's way of making sure his friends were safe and not on the streets.

Maurice would help his classmates with their homework so they would not fall behind. Maurice and his younger brother were both born in November a few years apart. We called him Doom or Stink, they shared the same name, Jr. He would often stay at our home. He thought he was hiding out in Maurice's room, but I knew. Maurice was the type of child that always kept me on my toes. I would always have to be ready to give him an explanation to his questions. "No" or "yes" was not good enough. The teachers loved him, they thought that he was the sweetest kid. He had a smile and a laugh that were out of this world. Maurice was the type of child that would call me the moment I left the house until I returned home. That was just him. He was a bug. I would always say, "I feel sorry for his girlfriend."

I will say, being raised in the house with all women, he knew how to treat a woman and clean a house. I had him standing in a chair at the kitchen sink, washing dishes, at an early age. My children rotated with chores in our home. Dishes, bathroom, vacuuming, living room, and rooms. My children knew our struggle and they did what they could to help. If Maurice found a dollar, he would bring that dollar home, just as proud, and give it to me. No, he was not perfect, he was just like the next child and did things that he was not supposed to do.

Maurice was a little guy for a long time. I remember there was one year when he sprouted up overnight. Because he was short, they would call him Little Man. He would work out as a child, building his muscles. I do believe that he had a short person's syndrome. He did not care how big you were, if you said something or did something, he was standing up for himself. Maurice was a fighter, and he would not back down. I would always tell Maurice, "No one fights fair anymore." Because he would not back down and would fight anyone, his life was taken. His life should not have ended like it did. Maurice loved sports and, as you already know, he loved the Pittsburgh Steelers. Maurice ran track, played baseball, football, and even tried playing soccer. I was afraid of him getting hurt playing sports, but guys that I knew told me to stop babying him and let him play. I am glad I did because he was good. He was extremely competitive, and he enjoyed it. Let me take you to that day.

The Call

Michelle

I remember that day just like it was yesterday. How could I ever forget? It was a call no parent wants to receive. You often see it on TV, but when it becomes a reality, there are some phone calls that will make you forget who you are and where you are. God is truly amazing because He set me up and called me to a 40-day prayer challenge before any of this would take place. God had me in a position of prayer when He knew I would need Him the most. It was prayer that saved my life. I am here to tell you I learned how to call on the name of Jesus. Even when I could not say a word, I knew God knew what was on my heart.

My friend, Charrell Felton, who I have been friends with since the fifth grade, is a reader, so she sent me a book. It was called *Draw the Circle Maker*, and she said she felt led to invite Pastor Dawn Michelle, who I did not know at the time. We all read the book and once we got done, we decided to do the 40-day prayer challenge. Pastor Dawn Michelle mentioned that she was going to invite someone else to join us, but they had mentioned on day ten of her prayer group, that the warfare was so great when they did the 40-day challenge, they did not continue with the challenge. Each morning, we got up and prayed at 5:00 a.m., discussed the book, wrote in our journals our prayer points for that day and what we wanted to circle in prayer and come in agreement with. One of the things each one of us did was draw a circle, sit in that circle, and meet God each day in prayer. I drew my circle in Maurice's room and each morning, I would go sit in the circle, and that is where I would meet God, pray, and journal after each call. God chose two women from Virginia Beach to stand beside me when I would experience the worst nightmare of my life. God knew I would need them. God gives you a lifeline. He knew I would not be able to handle this alone. On day ten of the prayer challenge, Pastor Dawn prayed that morning and her prayer was for gun violence and murder, suicide, and protection, etc. I will never forget my spirit cried out that morning, moaning and groaning. I was crying out of my spirit. I did not know then, but the spirit knew that my son would be murdered at 5:00 p.m. that evening.

Charrell called me after we got off the prayer call and she even questioned the cry I had. She told me that my cry was different from any other morning. I told her I was unsure as to what was going on, but I knew that Pastor Dawn Michelle was called to be our midwife and our purpose pusher. Her prayers were so powerful. I hung up the phone and I continued to pray while I drove to work. I felt uneasy and I remember asking God to save my son, and to protect and keep him.

I arrived at work around 7:30-8:00 a.m. I got my first call from Maurice. I talked to Maurice like 10-20 times that day. All day long, he would call me, and we would talk off and on. When my phone rang, it was Moe. There were some calls where he did not even want anything. During one of the calls, Maurice told me he had something he wanted to talk about once I arrived home. In another of our conversations, Moe asked me if he could move back home. I told him, "Yes," I would be okay with him coming home and getting himself together. I was happy my baby boy was coming home, and everything would be all right.

Another conversation we had that day involved him telling me that some guys were getting on his nerves, calling him a snitch, and saying that the truth would come out. The advice I gave my baby was to not worry about them. Little did I know about how the streets operated. My baby was scared. He knew in his heart that these young guys were serious; they carried guns and did not care. I believe my son knew he was leaving this Earth in a few hours. Maurice was a fighter, and he would give you a fair fight any time of the day.

Maurice called me around 3:00 p.m. to see if I was on my way home. I had decided to work a little overtime that day since Maurice said he was moving back home, and I wanted to make sure I had extra money to be able to help him get whatever he needed to put him in a good place. Maurice called me one more time and I said to myself, "He is really bugging me today." I thought he was being a bit extra and was really trying to butter me up and play with my heart.

I left work around 4:00 p.m. and I ran upstairs into Moe's room. I sat on his bed, waiting for him to call, or come to the house. I texted him, but received no answer, then I called and still no answer. I said to myself, "Where is he?" I turned on the television and I got this horrible feeling in my gut. I kept listening for the door or for my phone to ring. I was sitting on the bed, and I heard a siren and then my phone rang. It was Kwane on the other end of the phone. Kwane was one of Maurice's good friend's brothers. Kwane said, "Mom, Maurice has been shot. I need you to get to the hospital." I remember Kwane repeating himself to make sure I heard him, and he hung up. Immediately, I ran out of the house, and I do not know how I made it to the hospital, but I did. I called LaChae and Laurice and told them Moe was shot. I cannot remember who else I called or what I did, but when I got to the hospital, I beat the ambulance to the hospital again. How? I have no idea how, but I did. I saw them pull up and I knew that was my son on the inside. Every mother knows their child, especially when you have that connection. Even though he got on my nerves at times and did not listen, we still had that bond.

I went inside and told the registration desk that they were bringing my son in on the ambulance that was outside. I gave them Moe's name and informed them that he had been shot. They asked me to go to the family waiting room. From the experience that I had with my father, I knew that the family waiting room was not a good sign. LaChae, Laurice, Sharon, Kathy, and Karen were there, and I am not sure who else. The doctor came out and I knew right then, but she saw the look that was in my eyes because she said, "We are doing everything that we can do," and left out. There were so many different people who came to knock on the door who wanted to come in with the family. But I could not talk, nor did I want to talk to anyone. We all know that news travels and the streets talk, so we had so many people calling. Kwane never showed up, nor did Maurice Sr. No one from the Geter family was present that I can remember. The doctor came back in and said, "We have done all we can. Maurice is deceased."

I looked at the doctor and I asked her to take me to my son. I just believed at that moment that if I could touch my baby and pray for him, he would come back to life. The doctor expressed that with the way he was, she could not allow me to go back. I said, "Just clean him up, I need to see him." Her answer was still no. I dropped to the floor, and I began to cry like there was no tomorrow. Everything inside of me died at that very moment. My faith, my joy, my hope, my peace. I could not hear anything or anyone else for a period; I did not want to do anything. I was hurt. The pain I felt inside was a pain I had never experienced before. My Miracle Man was gone; my baby boy, my only son. Lord, how could this be? Maurice came into this world unexpectedly, and he left this world unexpectedly.

Maurice was the child that was not supposed to be here. But God had another plan. No one knows a mother's pain unless you have sat in my seat or walked in my shoes. I do not wish this on any parent or any family at ALL. I have all these thoughts running through my head. "Why would God allow this to happen? Why would He allow me to conceive a child, my baby child, my only son? Name him my Miracle Man and then, twenty-one years later, allow him to be snatched from me? Is this what we are doing, God?"

There was a young lady who they let in the room. The girl said Maurice rented a room at her mother's house. She came in, stating that the police were at her house and asked to see the room that Maurice stayed in. I was not sure why at the time, but I later found out that Maurice was gunned down in the alley next to the house he lived in. Chief Carter at the time stopped in to give his condolences. Mr. Ricky, Kwane's stepfather, came in and he prayed for Maurice. I listened to his prayer and at that moment, he had no clue that Maurice was no longer with us. He prayed for God to spare Moe and heal him. I do not even know how long we were in the waiting room. My nightmare had come true. I had to leave the hospital without my son. He was gone.

How would I get through this? I felt so lost. Why would someone do this to my baby? This was a different type of heartache that I never want to experience again. I carried him in my womb, and I can feel the pain to lose a child, and to a violent death does not make it easy. I went home and I bawled like a baby. I did not sleep at all that night. "How do I go on? What do I do?" I was a mother that felt so lost at that point. I was so excited because my son was moving back home, and we talked so many times that day. What if I would have avoided his phone calls? What if I was too busy to take time out to listen to what Moe had to say to me? My last conversation with him, I told him, "I love you and I will be home soon, and I will text you once I arrive home." What if I would not have taken his calls? What if I did not get a chance to tell my baby that I loved him? The feeling is so unexplainable, and I will probably take it to my grave. The loss of a child so suddenly and in such a violent way—my baby gunned down so close to home. A mother's worst nightmare became her reality.

I remember my mom coming out of the room and asking me what was wrong and why I was crying. I explained to her that Maurice was killed. Remember, my mother had Alzheimer's and Dementia at the time, and I could tell that she was trying to process everything I was telling her. My mom felt my pain that day. How do I hold back the tears? The muzzle just gripped me, and I did not have any more words. Maurice just celebrated his birthday four days ago. I rented him a car for his 21st birthday, gave him a card and money. Maurice's birthday is November 15th, his football Jersey was #15, he was gunned down on 15th street, and that year, he was Harrisburg's 15th homicide victim of 2014.

I waited until 5:00 a.m. on November 20, 2014. I got in my circle in Maurice's room, and I got on the prayer call the next morning and it was silent. Pastor Dawn Michelle and Charrell did not know what to say to me. I do not even believe they thought I would join the call. But I did, and I did not even know what to say to them. I did not know where the words came from, but I told them that morning that I needed them. I needed their help, their strength, and support, and that I could not have them be silent on me, not then. I needed them to come with the same strength and energy they had the first ten days of the prayer call. I believe it was my day to pray, but I do not recall praying. If I ever needed prayer, I needed the power of prayer to show up in my life. I had to do something to continue on. I did not know what else to do and to be honest, nor did I want to do anything else. I had never been in this place before. The loss of Maurice taught me to be consistent in prayer. It taught me how to call on God. It was when the intercessor/ prayer warrior was birthed.

We completed the 40-day prayer challenge, and it is still growing strong today. I learned how to pray through. I had to show up, even when I did not want to. So many scriptures became so alive during this time. I learned to know my sisters after the Spirit and not after the flesh. I am truly grateful to Pastor Dawn Michelle, the woman of God who did not know me, but she labored with me, prayed with me, cried with me, and loved me to life to get me to this place I am now. That is the love of God. Charrell Felton called me every day for an entire year to make sure I was good. That is a real friend. Even if Charrell did not know what to say, she made conversation. Charrell even came to visit me. She showed me what a sister keeper is (Yes, I am my sister's keeper). I am ever so grateful for the outlet and the support that God set me up with. So many women on the prayer call have supported and prayed me through. We have all had our moments in life and our time to cry. *Let the weak carry the strong*, and they did just that for me. People often ask me today how I made it, how I am still standing strong. It is the grace of God, and prayer, and prayer warriors. When you go through something that is so devastating, you need a good support system; those shoulders that you can lean on, so you do not find yourself in that dark place. We all grieve differently.

Miko Cherry, Macey Miales, Monique Belfield, Kathy Watson, Kathy Fayne, Kim Felton, Tonya Hall, Mom Myrtle Brown Kinard, Mom Brenda Whittaker, Prophet Josh Tucker, Zaymane Dawson, and a few others have all helped me at one time or another, and I thank God for Morning Glory Prayer call at 5:00 a.m. God's design alignment. No one could have done this but God. To God be all the glory! We laugh, cry, sing, talk, pray, and take trips together. The openness, transparency, and love have and is keeping us together and strong.

I do not know about you, but there were times when I thought I was about to lose my mind, trying to cope with the loss of Moe. I said, "God, if anything else happens, I do not know how I am going to be able to keep standing." But God really knows what is on the inside of us all. I really did not have time to have a *woe is me*, pity party. I had my mom, children, grandchildren, and those who loved me to think about. I am still trying to help everyone else when I really needed the help myself. I often think about, what if I would have never accepted the 40-day prayer challenge that I know for sure God was calling me to? What if Charrell had not been obedient to God or if Pastor Dawn Michelle was too busy? I know it may be a lot of what ifs. But what I learned is that it is so important to be led by the Spirit. I could be dead in my own grave, left God, addicted to drugs, out of my mind. Lord, I thank You, that You saw fit not to let me go when I wanted to let go. Because in my mind, I had all the reasons why I should or could sin. "God would understand," I thought to myself. I even thought about easing the pain through vengeance, drinking, fornication, wondering if I would feel better being in the arms of a man, and for a few minutes, would that make me feel better? If I did, how could God say anything to me? I have all the right and how dare He hold it against me? So many times, I would have to have a reality check with myself. Thank God I knew enough to call on the name of the Lord, and I had people praying for me. Some I knew, and some I did not know. Yes, I was praying, but at times, I was still in a dark place. Depression and loneliness began to grip my very soul. I had to begin to change my perspective and my confession. A better November to remember.

Where Do I Start?

LaChae

With my brother, I honestly still can't even believe that I have a sibling that died, especially because I'm the oldest. It just feels like this wasn't supposed to happen to us. Who would've thought that this would be our story? I mean, I'm sure every family that has experienced this feels the same way, but this is something that you never think will happen to you.

Me and Reese are six years apart, so it seemed like his sole purpose was to annoy me. We went back and forth all the time, so much that it wasn't even funny. I enjoyed getting him in trouble and telling on him every chance I got. I feel like the relationship my kids, Bryson and Mason, have is payback for how I was with Reese. Bryson just picks with Mason so bad, just like I used to do to my brother.

It was always just us three, LaChae, Laurice, and Maurice, that made up Michelle's kids. Michelle's kids are very similar to

Bebe's kids, except our mom's name is Michelle. With Reese being the youngest and the only boy, it felt like he got the most attention. As soon as he came along, it was all about him. My mom loved her son so much. I mean, I'm sure she loves us all, as she would say. I guess that's the politically correct answer, but as a mother of two boys, I know there is just something different about moms and their sons. We have home videos of Laurice and I that were recorded by my grandpa when my mom was in the hospital, and we were so excited to meet our little brother. When he came home, we made more videos with him and were so happy to have him.

Growing up, Reese was such a smart kid, and he had a really good memory. My grandma Rose was excellent, and she went over our schoolwork with us and read books to us. If you knew Rose's personality, you wouldn't expect this to be the case, but she really had a way with her about that. She didn't want us to be "no dummy," as she would say. She would teach us songs and everything; she was great about that. She did that with each one of us, including Reese. Whenever family would come over, Reese would "read" books to them before he had even started school. The funny thing was that he didn't really know how to read yet, Rose had just worked with him so much and his memory was so good that he had memorized his books. And boy, did he think he knew everything. But honestly, so did I, so that's why we butted heads so much. Now, don't get me wrong, we had a fair amount of time when we did get along. We seemed to like the same things and maybe part of that was because I was his big sister, and even though he didn't want to admit it, he looked up to me.

I remember one year for Christmas, we wanted the original PlayStation, you know, the gray one that had Crash Bandicoot on it. We both put together our Christmas money to buy the PlayStation and the games and we shared it. He also liked and appreciated my style. I knew how the young boys dressed at the time, and I would always pick out clothes for my mom to buy him or buy them myself when I got older. I remember this one year for Christmas, Laurice was trying to be different, and I told her he wasn't going to like the boots she picked out, but she got them anyway. I can't remember what kind, I think they were some Rocawear boots. They didn't look bad, they just weren't his style. I had bought him some regular Timbs and ACG boots. They were popular at the time and that was what he liked. I don't think he had the heart at first to tell her he didn't like them, but you could tell by his face that he wasn't feeling her gift. Me, being the instigator I am, came out and asked him and he finally admitted he didn't like them. He ended up giving them to Stephen, who wore the same size and was my boyfriend at the time. I have a bunch of Christmas stories because Christmas was our thing. Especially when we got older, we loved to come together and exchange gifts on Christmas morning.

One year, after we already had kids and I believe Laurice was pregnant with Elite, we weren't speaking to each other but we all still showed up to my mom's house on Christmas with gifts for each other and our kids. Reese came in dressed like Chubbs; they had a matching outfit and sneakers on. We all sat around, not really talking at first, and my mom kept trying to get us to talk. It wasn't until Bryson broke the ice by getting his butt on a toy that was supposed to be for Chubbs and riding on it like he was riding a horse at a rodeo. It was so funny that we all couldn't help but laugh. After that, my mom says to Reese, "Go and give your sister a hug." He looked at me with a smirk, like he knew he wanted to but didn't know if I would receive it, and he didn't want to be the first to break the ice. I remembered smiling back, and he did give me a hug, and we were cool again. After all, it was Christmas and Christmas was our thing. I do my best to keep the Christmas tradition going, no matter how I'm feeling or what mood I'm in that year. I want our kids to experience that same kind of Christmas and have those same memories.

Reese had his first son a few months after I had mine, and then Laurice wasn't too far behind with having Elite. I was big sis; I went down with him to the hospital the day that Chubbs was born to see the baby. He was mad because I was being "too Joe" with them people. But I just knew that Chubbs was his child, and I wasn't going to let him get away from his responsibilities. My mom was riding with her son, he said the baby wasn't his, so that's what she was going with, but as for me, I just knew. His son's mother had befriended me on social media, and I had read the messages in his phone with how he used to talk to her before she got pregnant. At the time, he was a popular McDevitt football player, so my mom thought she was trying to trap her son. At the end of the day, that was still my brother, so what did I do? I went with him to their house and swabbed the baby's cheek to take the DNA test because I was big sis. Again, right before Christmas, it came back that Chubbs was his son. We all went out and bought him all these gifts. That's the type of relationship we had. I was going to tell you if you were wrong, but still have your back.

At first, me and Laurice didn't think it was fair that my mom seemed to have gotten lenient with him. It would have been the end of the world if either of us would've had a baby in high school, but not for him. We had both moved out and Reese was getting away with stuff we would have never gotten away with at his age. Eventually, we kind of let it go and started letting him party with us. I remember he came to IUP for my graduation, and I let him stay at my apartment instead of going back to the hotel with the older people. He tried to be so cool, but he was so happy to say that he was at a college party. He would come over to me and my sister's house when we were having a get together and bring whoever was his friend at the time with him, and those were some times. Man, I wish we could re-live some of those days. He went away to Army National Guard, and I was proud of who he was becoming. But then things started to change.

He started hanging with the wrong people and being disrespectful. He stopped going to his National Guard commitments. He was going down the wrong path. He wasn't staying with my mom anymore. None of us had his number and if he wanted to talk to us, he would call blocked. He deleted us off of his social media, and he was mad that I would tell my mom what he was posting. So, we were in this weird space where we weren't really talking again. The last conversation I had with my brother was on September 11, 2014. That was the last time I heard his voice. It was my birthday. I was out at dinner and got a call from a blocked number and I answered it. It was Reese, calling to wish me a happy birthday. See, no matter what, even though I didn't agree with his actions, even though he thought I needed to stay out of his business, that was still my brother, and he knew he needed to call me on my birthday. On his birthday, I didn't have a number to call him because he wouldn't give it to us. So, I made a post for him on Facebook, even though we were no longer friends, because usually that gets back and they somehow get it, but it wasn't the same. I didn't get to talk to him on his birthday though, and this was a milestone birthday. He was turning twenty-one.

Four days later, on November 19, 2014, I went to work like I did any other day. I was working at Vantage Foods at the time, and had to be at work at 4:30 in the morning to inspect the lines before we started up. I remember that day being a really bad day. I was getting tired of my job and the hours, so I had recently went to interview for a Microbiologist position at my current job, which I later got. We had been having an issue with cube steak, and my days that were usually pretty chill and in the lab, had been spent on the floor, in the cold, moving around and inspecting pallets all day. I was so happy to be off of work and I was tired when I left around 4:30 p.m. from a 12-hour shift. I was not necessarily happy to go home, because me and Stephen, my now husband, were into it at the time and not really speaking, so things were also tense at home. I got home and took my shoes off and was scrolling on Facebook. I saw one of my friend's post, "Did anybody hear all those gunshots go off around 15th Street?" I kept scrolling, of course, I didn't think anything of it. Why would I? Shots go off all the time. Not long after, I got a call from Laurice. She said, "I just got off the phone with mom, I'm on the way to the hospital, she said Reese got shot." I told her to come and get me, and her and Eric, her husband, picked me up and we rode down to Harrisburg Hospital together. I think I told Stephen where I was going, but honestly, none of us were really too concerned.

Laurice's voice was calm for the most part when I talked to her. Yes, I know they said he had been shot, but still, it never crossed my mind that he wasn't okay. Honestly, I was mad as I rode to the hospital. I had worked twelve hours and Laurice said my mom was freaking out, which she always does, so that wasn't cause for alarm. I was on my way to that hospital to cuss my brother out for making my mom worry like this. Or so I thought. I later coincidentally found out that those shots that I read about on Facebook were directed at my only brother.

We got to the hospital, and they put us in this room. We were not in the emergency waiting room. Why not? I never even knew that room existed. My mom was in there, out of it, crying. She told us she got a call that she needed to get down to the hospital, so we were waiting. A black nurse or doctor came in and the look on her face made my heart drop. She had on scrubs, her lips were chapped, and she had tears forming in her eyes. She had a defeated look on her face, like she had just lost a fight, and she had. My mom was a mess before she could even finish delivering the news. I was in complete and utter shock. "This can't be true, let me in the room so I can wake him up and then cuss him out for playing like this." Those were my thoughts, but I never got to talk to him again. Well, I talk to him, but he no longer talks back.

We sat in that special room for far too long. People started hearing the news; somehow, bad news travels fast. We started getting calls and the Facebook posts started. I still, to this day, don't look at my memories from around that time, because reading all those messages and posts is hard to stomach. People started coming down to the hospital with their versions of what happened, it was all too much. This was the talk of the town, and everybody wanted to give their opinions and be Facebook detectives. When Chief Carter came, it made it official. He offered his condolences and assured us he would work to ensure the person responsible was captured. My brother's body was evidence and he recommended that we not see him until after the funeral home cleaned him up. "Wait, was my brother seriously going to a funeral home? We have to have a funeral for that little baby that my mom brought home from the hospital that we couldn't wait to meet?" My mind couldn't process that as the current reality.

It was a dark time for me, and I really should've stayed off Facebook. Remember, I'm big sis, so there I was, angry and arguing with everyone that said anything opposing my brother. I was even about to meet up and fight this girl, but my mom was so scared, and after what had just happened to my brother, I didn't want her to worry. Even though she had nothing to worry about, because I was going to whoop that girl for running her mouth, but I was too angry so I'm glad I didn't put my hands on her. Otherwise, who knows where I would be.

In the days leading up to the funeral, there were a lot of us playing detective and trying to figure out what happened. The biggest bomb was that Reese had another baby on the way. This time, the roles were reversed, and my mom welcomed the idea, and I didn't believe it until we got proof. It seems like for some reason, after a person passes, there is always a girl that pops up saying she's having a baby. I was also at a very angry stage of my grief. My reaction was to lash out and attack those around me. So, I didn't care that this girl was pregnant and had lost her boyfriend, I thought she was clout chasing. That couldn't have been farther from the truth, and she is now a part of the family, but that's how I was feeling at the time.

The funeral was packed, so much so they had to open up the balcony of the church. It was again at Mount Zion and handled by Wallace. The family wore red, and Reese was dressed in red as well. He wore a lot of red. I remember a day we saw him walking down the street from head to toe in red, down to the socks. We later found out he probably did that because he was color blind. We never knew until he went into the military, I just thought his style was a little tacky. Come to find out when he would argue us down about what color something was, he actually had a reason for being wrong.

Overall, the funeral was fine until they opened it up for reflections. My anger creeped back in. My mom's ex-husband decided to show up and try to make himself relevant and that annoyed me, but what took the cake was a grown woman that had on a summer outfit and open toed shoes in November. My friends and people sitting around me must've seen the steam coming out of my ears as they began rubbing my shoulders and trying to calm me down. The only thing that stopped me from dragging her off the podium was not wanting my mom and other family members to be disappointed about me tearing that funeral up. Instead, I decided to get up and say a few words, even though I hadn't planned to, and that made me feel better. Not long after the funeral, all the details were exposed, and all of the responsible parties were captured and put in jail.

I went through a really angry stage after my brother was killed. I lashed out at those around me, and my marriage suffered. My husband was supporting me the best way he knew how, but he has never been in my shoes. Somehow, I felt like he wasn't doing enough. I withdrew from him, and he didn't know what he had done to make me feel so detached. I had told him I didn't want to be with him anymore and we were not speaking most of the time. We went to counseling with my pastor at my husband's request, and that actually helped me look at things differently and see what the true cause of my anger was. I wanted him to fix it, for him to make me happy and make me feel better, and he couldn't do that because he couldn't bring my brother back. After the counseling, we got back on track. I later got pregnant with Mason, and I think that helped to repair our bond and give us new life to be excited about. We are still going strong to this day.

Days after I gave birth to Mason, the trial started. I had to leave my literally newborn baby, fresh from the hospital, with a family friend. There was no way I wasn't going to be there, so I carried my postpartum body down there each day. One day, I had to go to the bathroom because I had breast milk leaking through and soaking my shirt, but still, I persevered. The trial was like reliving the whole experience all over again. We had to deal with the family members of the accused giving us dirty looks and defending their actions. Tensions flared up and one of the family members approached my brother's friend in the courtroom. I got up in front of the court and gave an impact statement. All for the judge and jury to give them a slap on the wrist. As usual, after the initial drama and the trial wore off, most of those people that were around in the beginning just to be a part of something or posting him on Facebook for clout don't even mention his name anymore.

It's been seven years since my brother's death, and already one of the responsible parties has been released from his sentence. They had us meet with the parole board and pour our hearts out and give statements, all for it to mean nothing. He got a recommendation for release from the judge that sentenced him. Part of his stipulations for release were that he wasn't supposed to be in Harrisburg so that we didn't have to run into him. And guess who I saw one day last summer while leaving my cousin's house? Yup, he looked right at me looking at him. The criminal justice system failed and continues to fail us. My brother was not an angel and I'll be the first to admit it, but he did not deserve to die. This remains the toughest loss for me so far, because he was only twenty-one, and the way he was violently shot down, it's hard for me to believe that he didn't suffer. It had to be painful. "What were his thoughts while he was in those last moments?" These are all things that I think about when I get quiet, and my mind starts to wander. These days, we get enjoyment from making memories with his two sons, Chubbs and Tyreece, whom he never got the opportunity to meet. I always wonder what things would be like if he were here with them. But we will never know.

Reece

Laurice

I don't know about anyone else, but I know I used to think about what life would be like for me and my siblings when we got older. What type of grandparents we would be. We were supposed to grow old together, but that is not how our story played out. Maurice, Reece, Moe, Little man, Nook- Nook, he was different things to so many different people. I do not know why, but by us being the youngest, we had a love-hate relationship. I like to call it a typical sibling relationship.

I remember this one time; we were sitting in the dining room and Reece needed a haircut really bad. It was like a light switch went off in my head and I asked him if I could cut his hair for him. Initially, he stared at me like I was crazy for even asking him to practice on his head. After a few moments of me convincing him and hearing a few, "Naw brah, you tripping, you not touching my head," he finally gave in. I happily went to the bathroom to retrieve the clippers and of course, not knowing what I was doing, I went to work on his head. When I was finally finished, he had swirls, zigzags, patches, anything you could think of. I can honestly say his head looked like a child just played in it. Reece went to go look in the mirror and he was on fire, and I could not stop laughing. His head looked horrible, but I could not understand why he was so mad at me when he knew I did not know what I was doing. I had never cut anyone's hair a day before in my life, so why would he allow me to play in his head like that? My stomach started to hurt from laughing so hard but looking around the room, not only was my brother pissed, but my sister was also mad at me because her being the older sister, she did not like the fact that our younger brother was standing there, mad, with a crazy haircut that I did. She sat my brother down and attempted to correct the mess that I created. Yes, I am one of Michelle's kids.

Not only was I the annoying older sister, I was also his protector, and I did not play when it came to my brother. I remember receiving a phone call from my mom one day and she had specific instructions. She said, "Laurice, can you please go to Reece's school, he called me and said he feels as though his teacher is picking on him." I put my shoes on so quick and made it to his school in 2.5 seconds. Normally, upon entering the school, I would have stopped at the office, but I walked past the office and proceeded to his classroom. As soon as I entered the classroom, I could see Reece sitting there, annoyed, and I locked eyes with one of Reece's best friends, Khalid, and his eyes lit up with excitement because he knew it was about to go down—in my Kevin Hart voice. I cussed his teacher out so bad, and told her if I received another phone call, and if I had to walk back up to the school, she would be sorry. As I started to walk out of the classroom, I glanced over my shoulder to Reece and his friends, and they were sitting in the corner, cracking up. Granted, my mom did not tell me to do all of that, nor did she know the specifics, all she knew was that I got the job done. Yes, I am one of Michelle's Kids. Him being my younger brother, I felt it was necessary to protect him, even when we did not always see eye to eye. I felt as though I was the only one that could torment him. No one else was allowed to do that to my baby brother.

I remember the call I received from my mom like it was yesterday. My mom called me with a calm tone, and I could tell she had been crying. She informed me that Kwane called her and said my brother had been shot, and she needed to go to the hospital. She told me she tried to call LaChae, but she did not answer. I quickly gathered myself, not knowing what to do. My husband drove me to pick my sister up and we rode in complete silence; nobody said anything on our drive to the hospital. I felt this big knot in my stomach. I knew in my heart that it was not going to be good, but I said a silent prayer for God to allow me to cuss Reece out for giving us all a heart attack. We arrived at the Emergency Department and were ushered into a small room where we sat, waiting patiently, with my mom for answers. Not long after, the doctor entered the room looking tired and defeated as she uttered, "I am sorry. I tried everything, but there was nothing else I can do." He was gone. I felt so empty. I probably should not have, but I did question how God could or would allow someone that I spent every day with for eighteen years to be taken from me. So many feelings and emotions came at once. I just sat in silence.

I always knew my mom was a very strong woman, but at that very moment, she knew that I was not okay, so she made me come sit on her lap and she just hugged me. I was thinking to myself this lady just lost her only son, the Miracle Baby, as she called him. She called him a miracle because she had her tubes tied after having me, so she was not supposed to have any more kids, but she had Reece. It was like he was destined to be here. Why would God tease us with twenty-one years on Earth? Reece had a lot more living to do. For me, everything was a blur from the moment we received notification of his death, the funeral, and even after the funeral. I was waking up daily with my eyes swollen shut from crying all night. I was not eating. I was even pushing the one person away that loved my family and supported my family the most throughout this entire situation, and that was my spouse. It was never intentional, I just felt as though nobody understood my pain except my mother and sister. I remember being so low, depressed, and defeated. I called my mom one day, telling her I wanted to go speak with a psychic because I needed to know if Reece was okay. Already knowing what her response was going to be, she told me I should not allow any unwanted spirits in my life and that I needed to pull it together, and I did just that.

I think the turning point for me was seeing how strong and positive my mom was throughout the whole situation, and my nephews, Tyreece and Chubbs. They bring my family so much joy and laughter, and we always feel as though Reece is in the room. It is the littlest things they do that remind us so much of their dad. They are different, but alike in so many ways; the mannerisms, the looks, the laughs, the jokes, and being very competitive. Like father, like son. Reece definitely left us with reminders of him through them. No longer can we play our family game, "You Are Not One of Michelle's Kids," with Reece, but he definitely was one of Michelle's kids. To know Reece was to love him.

Real Reece - **R**emember **E**veryone **A**int **L**oyal!

Don't Judge Me

Michelle

"I lost my two-year-old daughter when she choked on a piece of candy. I lost my two twins and my boyfriend in a car accident. I lost my dad when he set himself on fire in his car. I lost my fiancé one night in bed; he rolled over and passed away right beside me. My son is incarcerated for defending a friend. From the football field to a jail cell. I lost my mother while I was in high school; she was only in her twenties. I lost my mother in high school, and now I am forced to sell drugs to survive. My father was murdered while I was still in the womb and sometimes, I act out. My father was murdered when I was two years old, and sometimes, I am disrespectful and angry. My fiancé went missing a few days before our wedding, later I find out he is addicted to drugs. My husband was hit by a garbage truck, in a coma for months, and when he recovered, his memory was not the same, and neither *is our marriage. The man I love took everything I had. I watched my uncle beat my aunt to death.*"

We never understand sometimes what pushes a person over the edge or why a person acts the way that they do or does the things they do. I am not justifying a person's bad behavior or wrong choices that they make. But I do believe there are things lying beneath the surface. When you see that sister who is promiscuous, running from man to man, or even that young girl lost, trying to find love in so many different places. When you see that person addicted to drugs or that alcoholic, and they seem to be just drinking their life away. Even that person that has shut down and is quiet, you may say she or he is standoffish or acting funny. What about that young lady or young man that seem to be having an identity problem? What about that young man that sells drugs just to survive? It is not what he wants to do, but what he knows to do. Often, people suppress their feelings and do not know how to deal with the trauma, pain, guilt, and even shame, and they begin to act out or shut down. Some turn to the streets or even things that make them feel better for a moment. You get stuck in the pain, hurt, and guilt and do not know how to move forward.

"Stop judging me and come help me. Ask me if I am okay and what you can do to help me. I am not a bad person; I am just lost or lost my way. I do not want to drink, but I find myself drinking. I do not want that man or woman, but I find comfort in his or her arms. Help me, don't be afraid of me. I am just hurt, I am crying out, but no one can hear me crying. Can you see what is really behind my smile? I smile and joke a lot to hide my pain. You're complaining about traffic being backed up or not getting a promotion, and I do not have food on my table to eat. I lost all six of my kids in a house fire, that is why you see me out every night. They took all my children because I lost my job and I couldn't afford to keep up with the rent, that is why you see me on the pole dancing for money; I am trying to get my children back. You talk about me, but I really do not want to be here. I did not get to meet my father because they murdered him. I do not know how to manage my emotions. I am not bad; I just want my dad."

So often we judge the little boy on the streets, the women on the corner, because we really do not know their story. Next time you see that person that is struggling, don't judge them. Pray for them. Have compassion for them. *"Do not judge me, because you could be me or once was me."* We never know what situation in life can cause us to do wrong things or make us take a wrong turn down a dark path. We are so quick to sit in the judgement seat when we have all been in a bad place at one time or another or have done something wrong that we should not have done. The truth is, we just did not get caught. We often say what we will or will not do. It is not until it happens to you, and you must go through some of the toughest challenges in life. When life gives you a reality check, you begin to change your perspective and see things from a different lens.

"Yes, I have made a mistake, I know that I messed up. Don't judge me. 'Mother, why do you weep?' I weep because no one knows the pain I am going through. The sleepless nights, the tears I have cried, the things I had to sacrifice, the times I had to go without. The times I had to stand alone. The embarrassment, shame, and guilt I have carried around and had to live through. The days I carried an empty lunch bag to work, believing God that someone would give me lunch, which would actually be my dinner for the night. So often people look at where I am now and do not know where I have been or what it took for me to get here. Don't judge me, because you do not know my entire story. I told you a small fraction and you used it against me. You told me that you understood and cared, but when I needed you, you turned your back on me because you could not handle my truth."

We often pass judgment on a person because of what they look like or where they have been or done, or because we may even feel as if we are better than the individual. So often we say, "Do not judge a book by its cover." I totally agree; until you open the book and begin to read the story, looks are deceiving. These are sayings that have never lied. Just recently, I supported an organization called Heeding God's Call, that does a t-shirt memorial to those who lost their lives to gun violence. I remember the first time I helped and had to put a t-shirt on a pole for my son in 2015. It was hurtful and it was as if I had to dress my son. Well, this year, the memorial was from 2018-2023. It was sad to see the baby's t-shirt on the pole. What really shook me, right when I thought I was all good, was this young lady and her son standing next to one of the t-shirts, and she was taking pictures of her son. The little guy leaned over and kissed the t-shirt, and the mother told us that was his dad. I watched Kathy walk away and Iris hold back the tears. Others may not understand why I take the time and pride in hanging the t-shirts; it is because I am dressing that soul that lost their life and praying for those they left behind. Don't judge me, that is one of the reasons I weep.

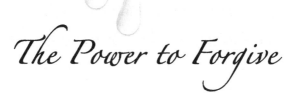

The Power to Forgive

Michelle

Forgive- "stop feeling angry or resentful toward (someone) for an offense, flaw, or mistake.[3] ". . .an intentional decision to let go of resentment and anger."[4]

When God say forgive, he means to forgive, let it ALL go. Whew. How do I forgive those who murdered my son? The young men that caused all this pain to my family? LaChae and Stephen are not getting along. Eric and Laurice seem to be at odds. Eric got in an accident and totaled his car and injured his back. The night that we laid Maurice to rest, two guys broke into my house, but did not harm me or my mother. December 26,

---

[3] Google.com. (n.d.). Forgive. In *Oxford Languages Dictionary*. Retrieved October 28, 2023, from Google.com search "forgive."

[4] Mayo Clinic Staff. (2023, Oct 28). *Forgiveness: Letting go of grudges and bitterness*. Mayo Clinic. https://www.mayoclinic.org/healthy-lifestyle/adult-health/in-depth/forgiveness/art-20047692#:~:text=Forgiveness%20means%20different%20things%20to,that%20act's%20grip%20on%20you.

2014, my divorce was final. A few people who were once in my inner circle ghost me when I needed them the most. Maurice Sr. has the nerve to blame me for Maurice's death. Imagine that, and he has the nerve to allow the words to come out of his mouth. My son's grandmother does not show up to her grandson's funeral. My family is not speaking to me. I did not know the judicial system, so the trial did not go the way I expected because of the decision I made to go to trial instead of accepting a plea.

There is just so much that seems to have weighed me down. But the biggest of them all is unforgiveness. How could I walk around with unforgiveness when God has forgiven me of so much? I remember hearing during the trial that one of the young men drove his girlfriend to work, went to the mall, and went shopping after he murdered my son. I thought about all the nights that I sat up going online to see if they had been caught and if their names were added to the Dauphin County prison inmate list. I was even angry at the police officers at one point, because it was not them that solved the murder or knew the whereabouts of the killers, it was Mr. & Mrs. Soto, Kwane's mom and dad. They should have had their own detective agency. I am ever so grateful for them. They always treated

Maurice like a son, and I did the same with Kwane. I treated Kwane like one of my sons.

I have my days and even my moments. I am human. But if I could encourage another mother, father, sister, sibling, anyone that has gone through what I went through or something similar, the biggest thing is you must forgive to move forward. I had to forgive all of them, everybody who I thought did me wrong. I had to earnestly pray that no harm would come to the young men and that justice would be served, even during the trial when it did not go the way I thought it would go. I had to believe God when He said, ". . .vengeance is mine. . ." (KJV, Romans 12:19). I had to even forgive the jurors, the parole board, and the judge. Even today, with how the system has failed my family. I cannot hold on to what has happened. Once I surrendered it all over to God, I began to be at peace. God has the final say so about everything. I know it is hard to forgive and it is a process. We start with the words on our lips, and then it must enter our mind and our heart. We often think that it is a cliche that *forgiveness is for us, not the other person or persons,* but it is true. When you forgive, you just begin to feel so much lighter.

I often remind myself that God is too wise to make a mistake. I know that I must answer to God. Lord knows I do not want my prayers being hindered because I had unforgiveness down in the crevices of my heart. God will never ask me about them, but about me. I had to also learn *how* to forgive myself. I walked around with regret, guilt, and shame, blaming myself for the things that had happened. Wondering what I did wrong, what I could have done different. I even beat myself up for not coming home sooner that day, questioning if I should have moved to the neighborhood I live in. Could I have been a better mother?

Sometimes, it is so hard to forgive yourself. That one that stares back at you every time you look in the mirror. Crazy, but I even had to ask God to forgive God, because I thought He was wrong. I also had to repent and tell God I was sorry and that I trust Him. Whatever you may be holding onto, whoever you may be holding onto, you must let it go or let them go. Do not allow the thing you are holding in your heart to manifest into disease. Going through so much, I kept saying, "I forgive, and I am letting it go," but I often found myself picking it or them back up. I remember after my brother, Mack Jr., passed, I had a mammogram scheduled that Saturday. When I went, they said they saw something in one of my breasts. I went back the next year and they said they saw something in both breasts. The devil is a whole liar, and the truth is not in him. Well, today, I can say that nothing was found in either breast. Release yourself, release them, and let it go.

I remember Mase had a song out that said, "breath, stretch, shake, let it go."[5] Whatever your IT is, let it go. You must do exactly that. No one is worth dying and going to hell over. Yes, it hurts. Yes, your life will never be the same again, but God allows us the grace to grieve. He strengthens us day by day, and He will put a path of people in your life that will help you all the way if you let Him. It is not easy, but I stand today letting you know it can be done. I am not bitter or angry. I am healthy, healed, and a whole mom. It did not happen overnight, and it is a process, but you must make up your mind that you want to put the work in. It is worth the work. I choose to be happy!

I owe a great deal to the best daughters in the entire world. My daughters, LaChae and Laurice, are my *ride or lifers*. I would not have made it through without them by my side. There were many days when they stepped up to the plate and did what needed to be done in every rough time while they were trying to grieve themselves. They stepped up with the holidays; one does Christmas and the other took over doing Thanksgiving. I have not had any type of celebration at my house since Maurice passed. We come together for my mom's birthday, or they may

---

[5] Mase. (2004). Breathe, Stretch, Shake.

drop by to drop off gifts, but that is all. They even allow Tyreece and Chubbs, Maurice's two sons, to spend time with their children often. Their husbands, Stephen and Eric, have stepped up with their nephews, interacting with them and including them in different outings. My grandchildren bring so much joy, laughter, and youthfulness to my life.

Losing Maurice really made me look at life differently and made me appreciate my girls and family. I still get upset, but I try not to hold onto it for too long because we never know what tomorrow will bring. LaChae and Laurice and their families give me a reason to smile. I try to ease up on them, but with the loss of a child it is hard at times for me not to be overprotective. There have been times when I get a phone call from them, and my heart just starts pounding or I will start the conversation out with, "What is wrong?" But I am getting better. They are my best friends. I am proud of the women they have grown up to be. It is their words and actions that have gotten me through some rough nights. If I call, they are there with no hesitation.

Things are still sensitive for all of us, but we have learned to lean on one another. We have learned to pull together. I owe them a lot. I am still learning to take their feelings into consideration. I lost a son, but they lost a brother. I lost a father, but they lost a grandpop. I lost my mother, and they lost a Rose. They had to deal with the pain just as well as I did. We have all learned from each other. They ain't one of Michelle's kids if they do not keep holding on… Love you, Laurice and LaChae. I appreciate and thank God, because I often think about what if Maurice would have been home and they murdered him at the house. Maybe my reactions would have been different, or the outcome could have been different. Even though I wanted to see him once he was shot. God knows best and that might have been something I could not have handled. I know there have been several times when I have been at church and I could see my father, mother, and my son laying in the front of the church, and I still can to this very day. Forgive, and God will take care of the rest. It lightens the load. Not only do you feel better, but you look better. *I forgive you for what you have done. Please forgive me!*

Mother, Why Are You Weeping?

A Special Thank You

Thank you to anyone who prayed for me, pushed me, supported me, encouraged me, was patient with me, covered me, stood by me, listened to me, heard my heart. Thank you for every act of kindness, and all those who showed me love and mercy. I thank God that He allowed me to open up to share part of my story. There were several times I wanted to erase what was written, but God said, "No, share your story."

A thank you to ALL of my family. A thank you to ALL of my Sister Circles of friends who have helped me through the process. Thank you to The All Nations Admin Team for all the tears and praises we shared in the office. Thank you Elder Reginald Frison and Carol Frison and the Mt. Zion Church Family. Thank you Apostle Melvin Thompson and Charese Thompson and All Nations Church Family. Thank you Paster Dawn Michelle and BOD Breaking of Day along with Morning Glory 5 a.m. Prayer Warriors.

Thank you Charrell Felton, for always being a friend. There has been no distance that has stopped you from coming to see about me.

Thank you, Kathy Watson; you are like my Peter in the bible, who has my back no matter what, who covers and protects me. Kathy Watson was dealing with her own storm but was right by my side; she was in one courtroom, and I was in another. Through this entire process, she has been right there.

Thank you, Sharon Staff, who is loyal for life as a friend and sister. Sharon showed me what genuine love was when she stepped up and cared for my mom like she was her own mother.

Thank you, Iris White and Charlotte Charles, who I can look at and never have to say a word, and who loved me without asking questions.

Thank you, Charis Grace Publishing, for all the support and making this an easy process.

I would like to thank Chase Snavely, Mindset Media, for designing the front and back cover of this book.

Thank you, Prophetess Traci and Women Gone Warrior Network. Thank you for the Push. God said, "If not NOW, then WHEN?"

Whoever purchases or reads this book, I pray that these words will help you or someone close to you.

A special thank you to my two sons, Stephen Morton and Eric Brickus. A mother could not ask for better sons for her daughters than the two of you, who have each proven to be great fathers, husbands, and even uncles. You have weathered the storms with us. I am proud to be called mom, mother, mom dukes, and even Sis. Michelle. A special thank you to my two beautiful daughters, LaChae Morton and Laurice Brickus, who opened up and decided to write this book with me. I believe it was healing for all three of us. I love you ladies.

What I will leave you with is:

> *Remember, don't be so quick to judge. We just never know what that person standing next to us has gone through or is going through. You will never understand my praise if you don't know what I have gone through. It's my praise that kept me in my right mind. My story may not be your story, but WE all have a story to tell. Tell your story!*

Peace and blessings to all those who will read this book.

About the Authors

A Mother and Daughter Trio

We are three women from a family who experienced the same losses, yet we continue to stand together in love, unity, understanding, and compassion. We leaned on one another for support and strength, while at times not understanding why or how we were going to make it through the storms. We saw the hurt and pain in one another and didn't always know what to say or even do at times. So, we decided to come together as *one* to share our story. It was not an easy thing to do, but it brought healing to our souls. We value our support system.

"Don't Stop Living, Loving, Laughing, and Learning Life's Lessons"

LaChae Morton   Michelle Geter   Laurice Brickus

Made in the USA
Middletown, DE
15 November 2023